Yan Zhenqing "Duo Bao Ta" Regular Script Copybook

颜真卿《多宝塔》

正楷大字帖

（九宫格式）

徐英才　徐英胜　编著

Xu Yingcai　Xu Yingsheng

Chicago Academic Press

Yan Zhenqing "Duo Bao Ta" Regular Script Copybook
Authors: Yingcai Xu and Yingsheng Xu
Publisher: Chicago Academic Press, November 23, 2020
First Edition: June 5, 2018
Second Edition: January 8, 2020
ISBN 9781719551311

书　名　颜真卿《多宝塔》正楷大字帖
主　编　徐英才、徐英胜
出版社　芝加哥学术出版社
2018 年 6 月 5 日第一版
2020 年 1 月 8 日第二版
书　号　9781719551311

Publishing　Chicago Academic Press
　　　　　　3811 Chester Drive
　　　　　　Glenview IL60026
E-mail　　contact@chicagoacademicpress.com
Website　　http://chicagoacademicpress.com/

Book Size　8.5X11 inches

目 录
Table of Contents

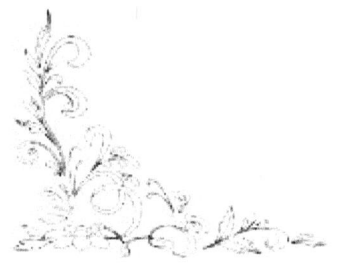
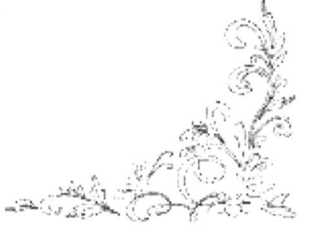

前　言

本字帖的最大特点之一是，字字均从楷书四大家之一的颜真卿《多宝塔》碑文的真迹里选编而成，从而能够让使用者一开始就学到地道正宗的颜体。

本字帖的第二大特点是，专为课堂教学设计，虽然它也可被用作自学教材。比如，为了便于教学，"基本笔法"一章的选字就坚持一字一画的原则。所谓一字一画，就是说，每个所选字内只出现一个待教的笔画而没有其他未教笔画来打扰。

本字帖的第三大特点是，在基本笔画和变化笔画后，还根据偏旁部首集结了例字，这样，学习者在学完基本笔画和变化笔画后，还可以集中学习偏旁部首的书写，为最后脱帖书写打下基础。

本帖还编有中国古代名句，以助学生在学期快结束时创作自己的书法艺术品。

另外，本字帖每个选字都给出了该字的汉语拼音和英语注解，这样，使用者在学习书法的同时还可以学习汉语，并知道自己所写究竟为何汉字。

Preface

The most important feature of this calligraphy copybook is that every character is chosen from the authentic rubbings of *Duo Bao Ta* by Yan Zhenqing, one of the four famous regular-script masters. Because of this, users can begin their calligraphy practice with genuine Yan.

The second important feature of this copybook is that it is designed particularly for classroom teaching use, although it can also be used as a self-study material. For example, to meet the need of calligraphy teaching, in choosing the characters for the chapter of "Basic Strokes," this book has adopted what's called the one-new-stroke-per-character principle. This means, each character in this chapter contains only one untaught stroke. This way, teachers can focus on the teaching of only one stroke per time.

The third feature is that, following the chapters on "Basic Strokes" and "Varied Strokes," characters chosen are arranged by radicals. This way, users, after learning the skills of writing the basic and varied strokes, can focus on the practice of radicals, as a preparation for finally writing without looking at the copybook.

Compiled in this copybook are also some famous sayings, which are designed to help users create their own artworks toward the end of their calligraphy course.

Last but not the least, all the characters chosen here are given Hanyu Pinyin and English definitions so that users can study Chinese language while studying Chinese calligraphy. This way, they do not write blindly, but know what they write.

说明：

　　本字帖所选每个字都给出了必要注解，其排列如下："该字的繁体形式＝该字的简体形式/拼音/英语"。比如十二页上的"會"字，其从左到右的排列是：會＝会/huì/meeting，其中的"會"是该字的繁体形式，"会"是该字的简体形式，"huì"是该字的汉语拼音，"meeting"是该字的英语定义。当然，如果该字没有繁体形式，繁体形式一栏就省略了。

　　本字帖所选每条"古代名言"都给出了数字编号。比如 1—A，则表示这是该名言的前半句；1—B，则表示这是该名言的后半句。如果仅给出了数字而没有字母，则表示这个名言单独成句。

Explanation:

　　All characters chosen here are given necessary notes. Below is how the notes are arranged: "The Character's Traditional Form = the Character's Simplified Form/Chinese Hanyu Pinyin/English Definition." Take the character "會" on page 12 for example. Arranged from left to right are: 會＝会/huì/meeting. Here "會" is the traditional form of this character, "会" the simplified form of the character, "huì" the Chinese Hanyu Pinyin of the character, and "meeting" the English definition of the character. If there is no traditional form of the character, then, of course, the traditional part is omitted.

　　In addition, numbers are given to index each famous Chinese saying. For exam, 1－A means the first half of the first saying; 1－B the second half of the first saying. If only a number is given without any English letter, that means this saying stands alone by itself.

基本笔法
Basic Strokes

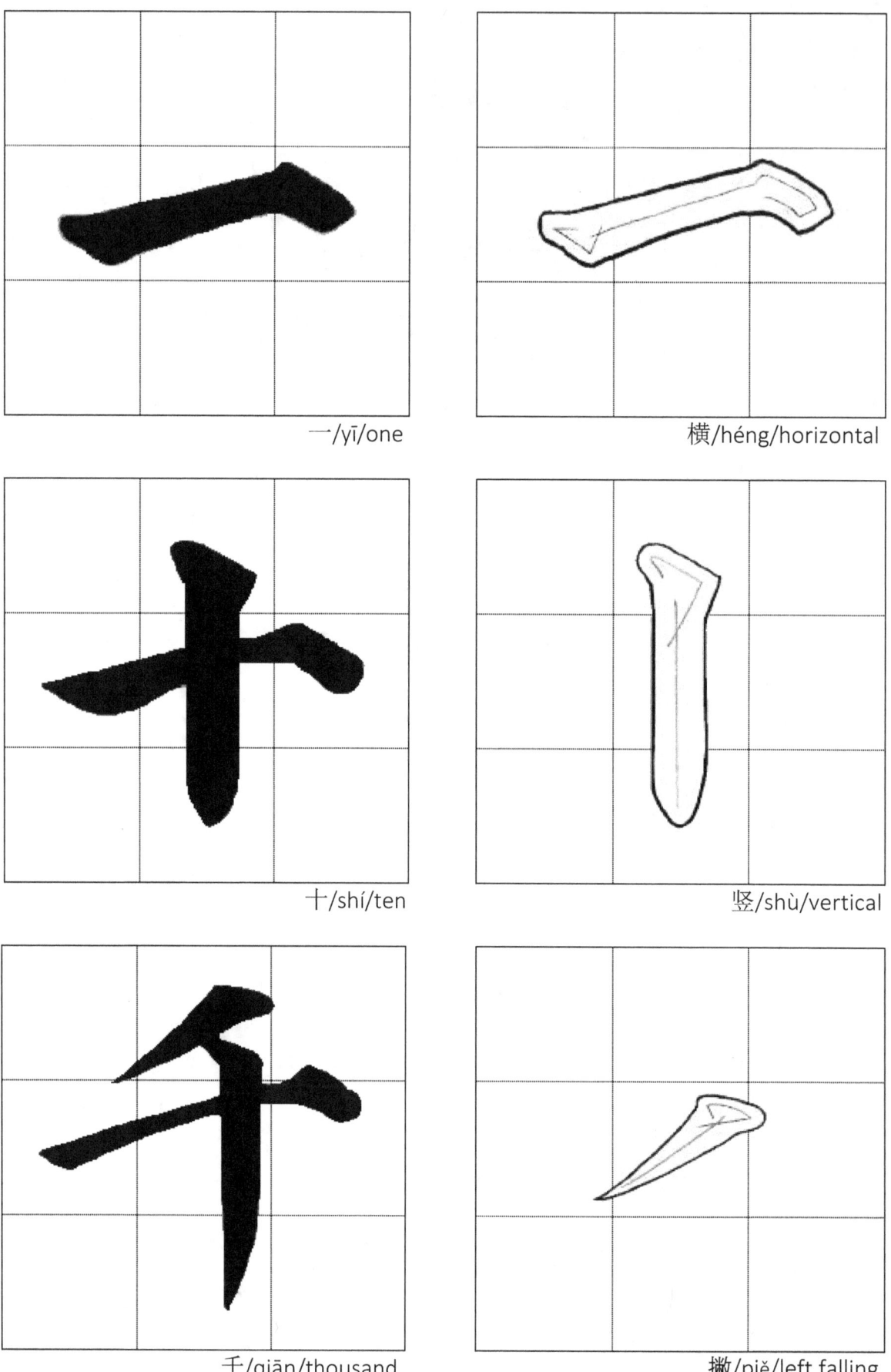

一/yī/one

横/héng/horizontal

十/shí/ten

竖/shù/vertical

千/qiān/thousand

撇/piě/left falling

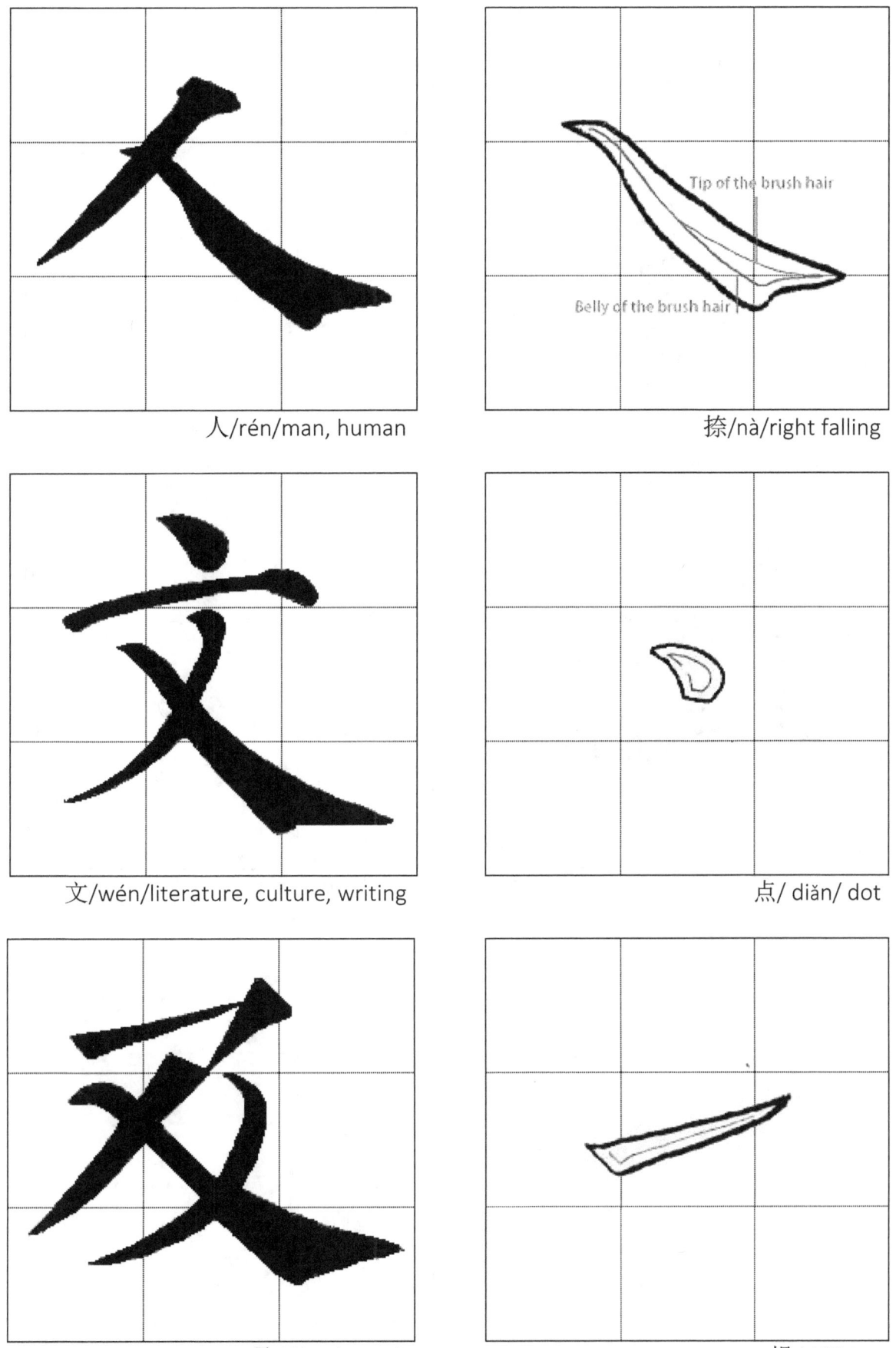

人/rén/man, human

捺/nà/right falling

Tip of the brush hair

Belly of the brush hair

文/wén/literature, culture, writing

点/ diǎn/ dot

及/jí/and, reach

提/tí/lifting

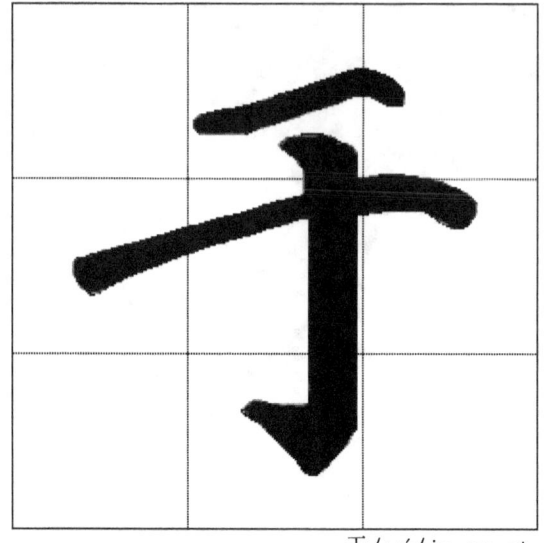

于/ yú/ in, on, at

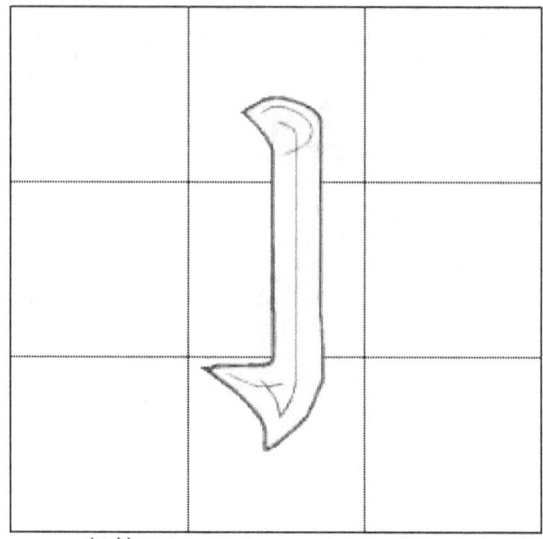

竖钩/ shùgōu/vertical turning to a hook

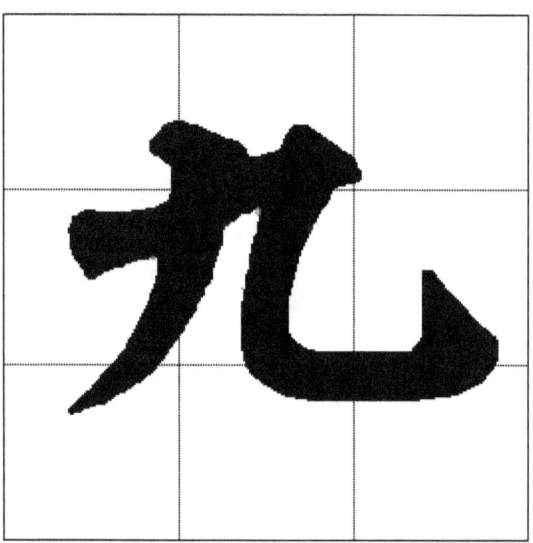

九/ jiǔ/nine

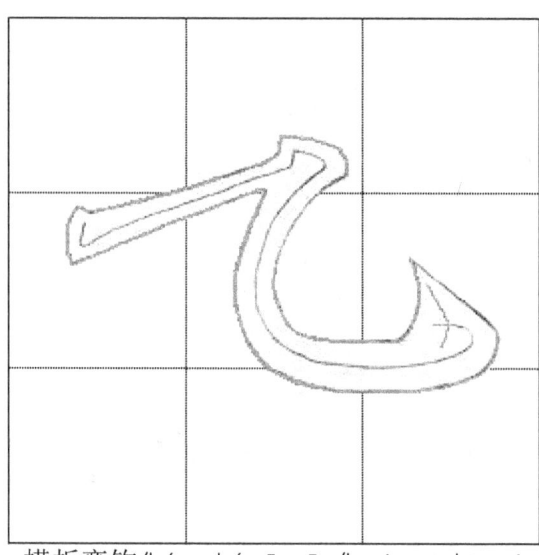

横折弯钩/héngzhéwāngōu/horizontal turning
to vertical to horizontal and to a hook

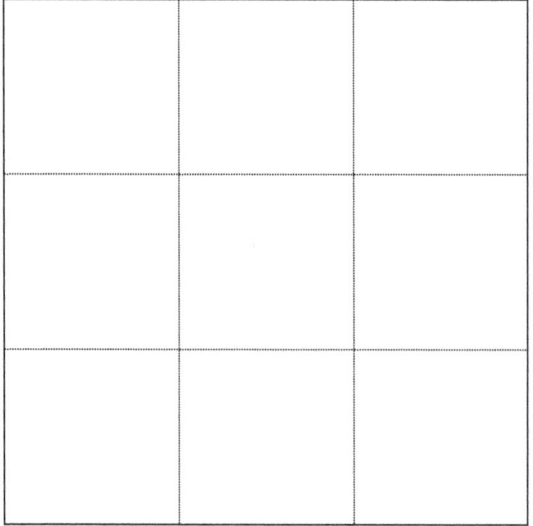

变化笔法
Varied Strokes

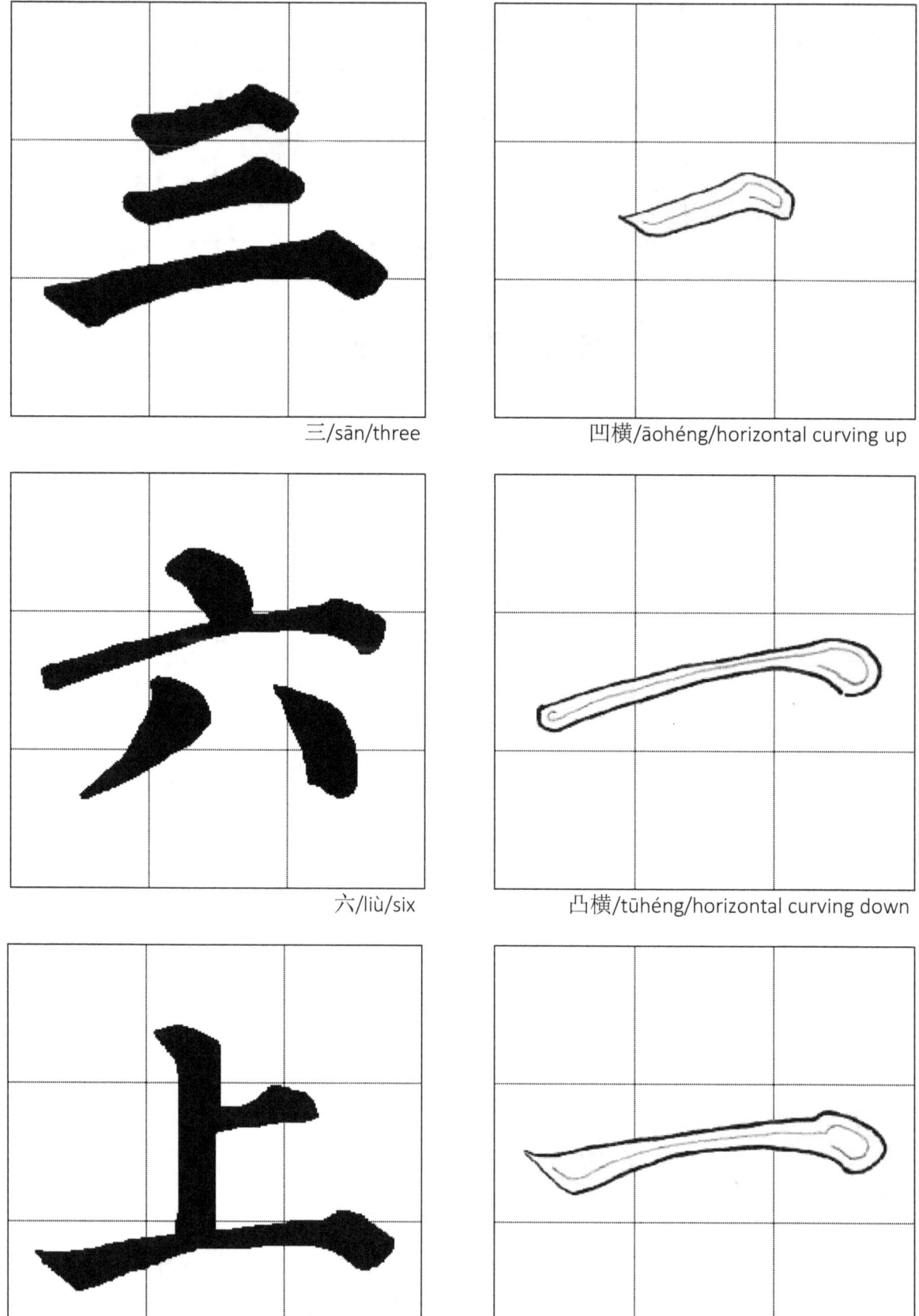

三/sān/three

凹横/āohéng/horizontal curving up

六/liù/six

凸横/tūhéng/horizontal curving down

上/shàng/up, top, ascend

细腰横/xìyāohéng/center-narrowed horizontal

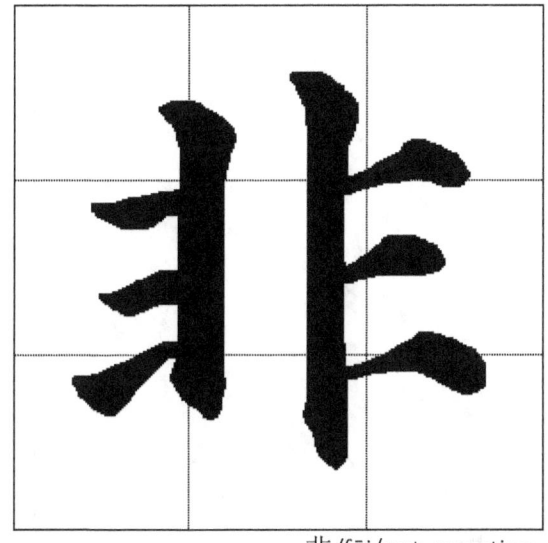

非/fēi/not, negative

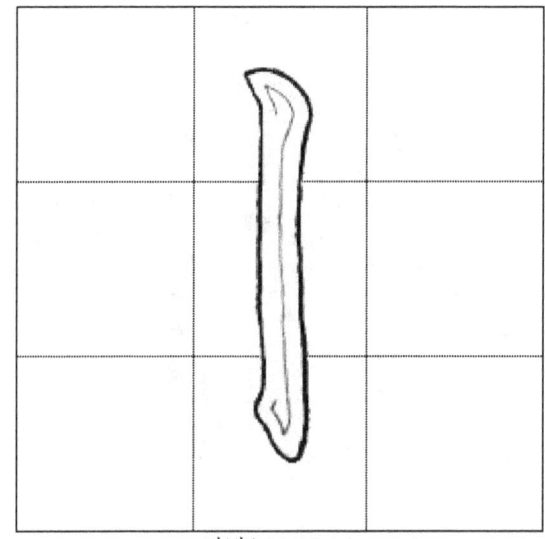

直竖/zhíshù/straight vertical

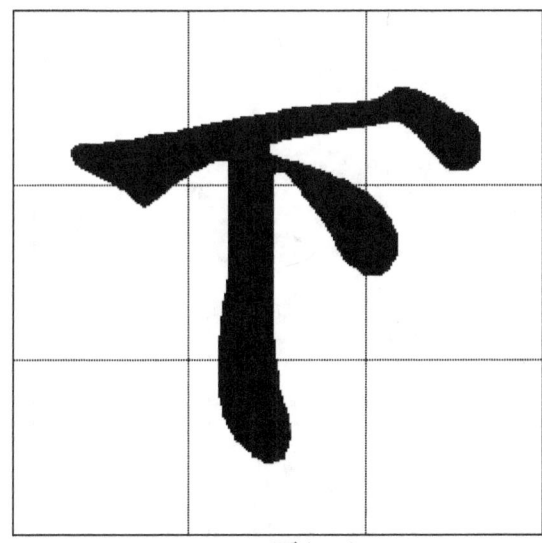

下/xià/down, descend

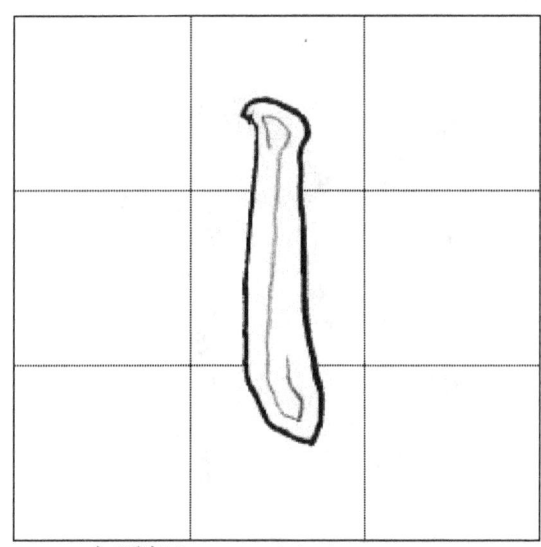

左弧竖/zuǒhúshù/vertical curving right

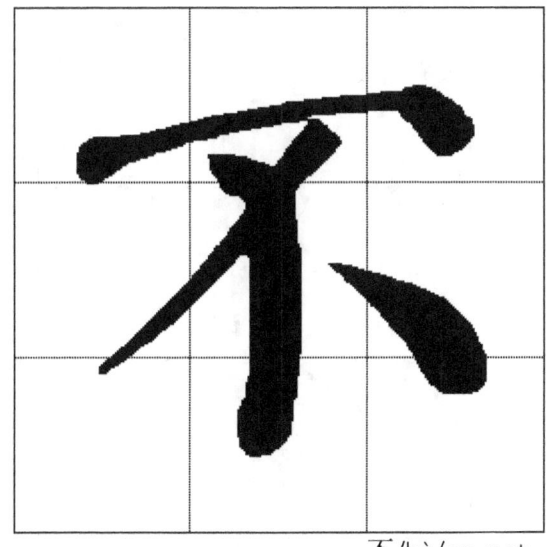

不/bù/no, not

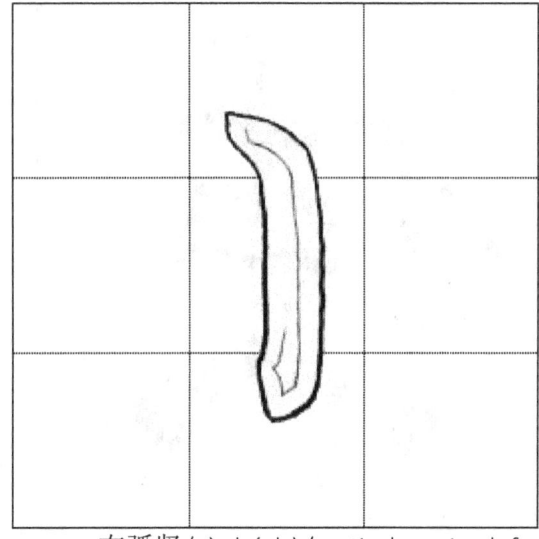

右弧竖/yòuhúshù/vertical curving left

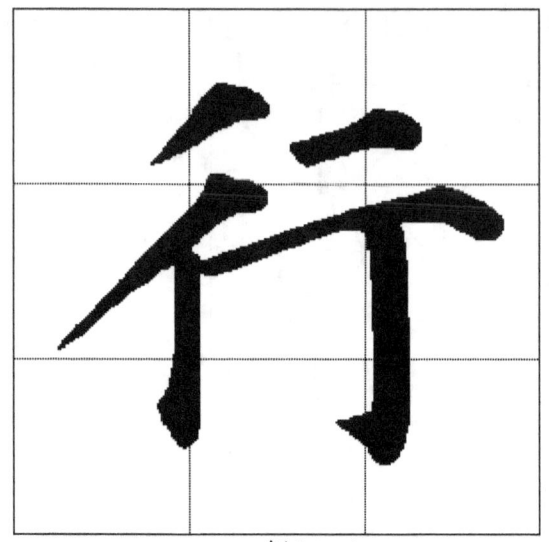

行/xíng/go, walk, move

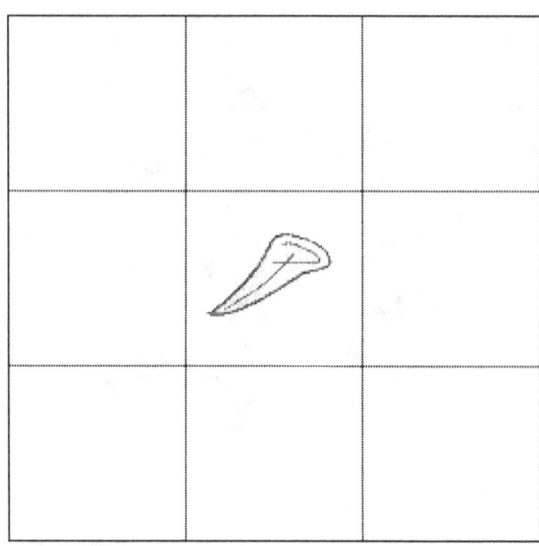

左下撇/zuǒxiàpiě/left falling that curves up

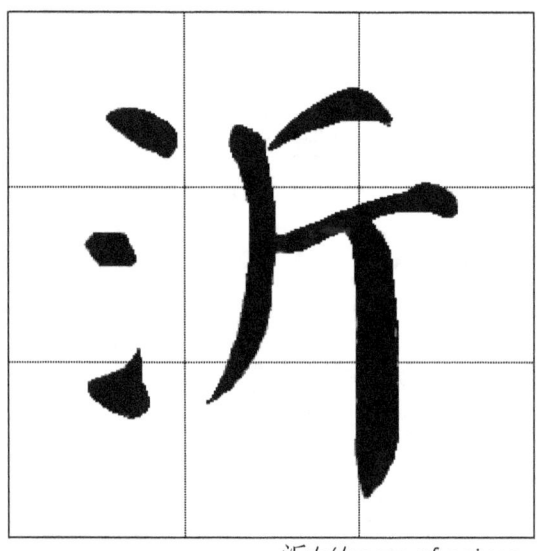

沂/yí/name of a river

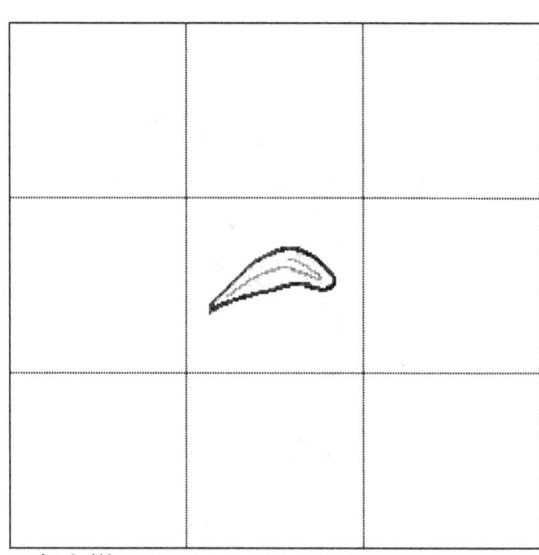

左上撇/zuǒshàngpiě/left falling that curves down

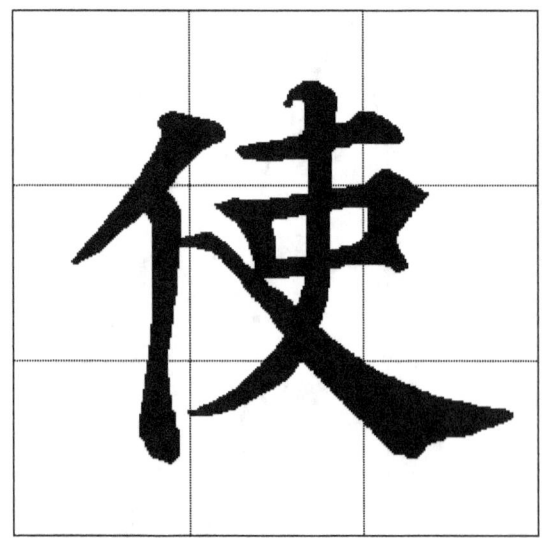

使/shǐ/make or cause sth to do

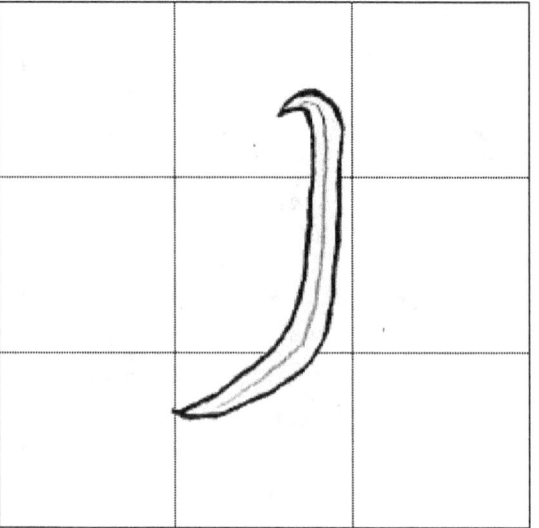

弧撇/húpiě/curved left-falling

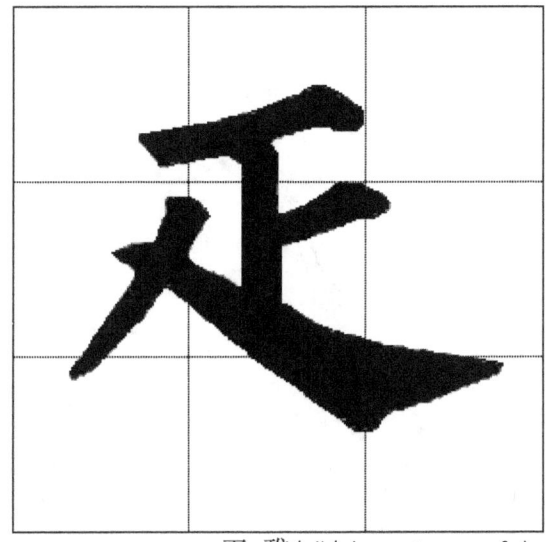

疋=雅/yǎ/elegant, graceful

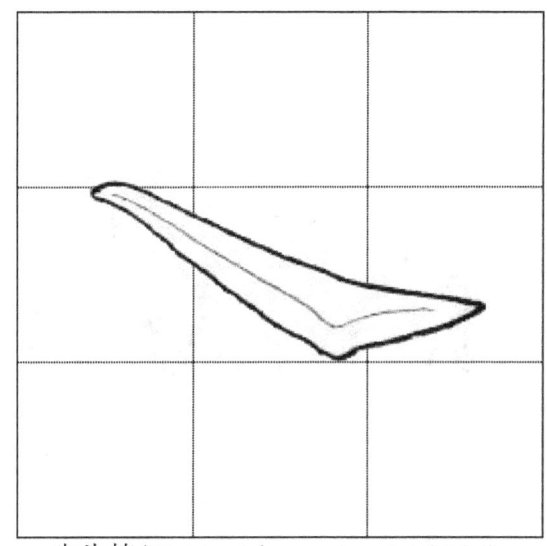

尖头捺/jiāntóunà/arrow-head right falling

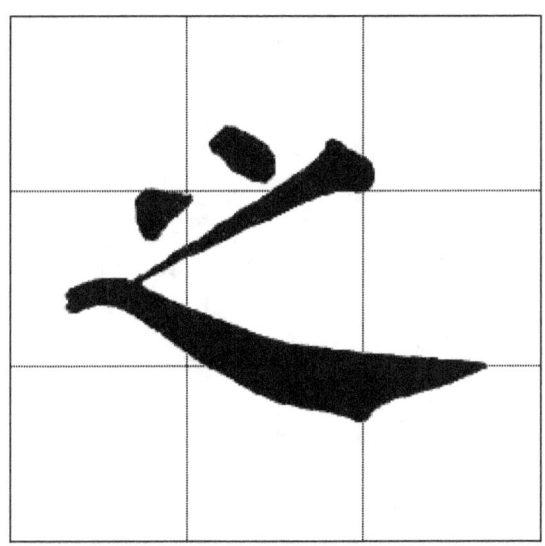

之/zhī/'s, of

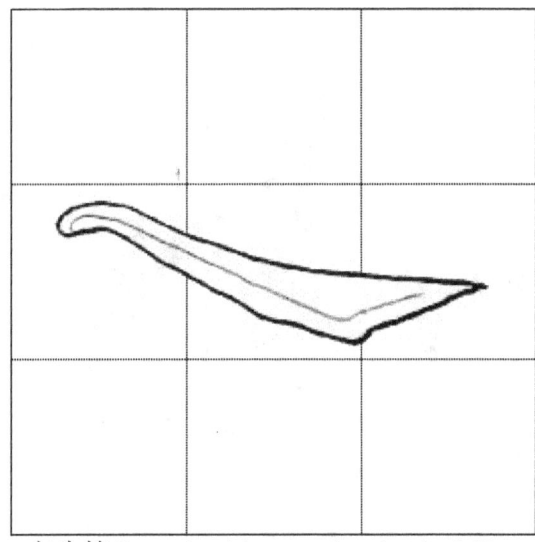

方头捺/fāngtóunà/square-head right falling

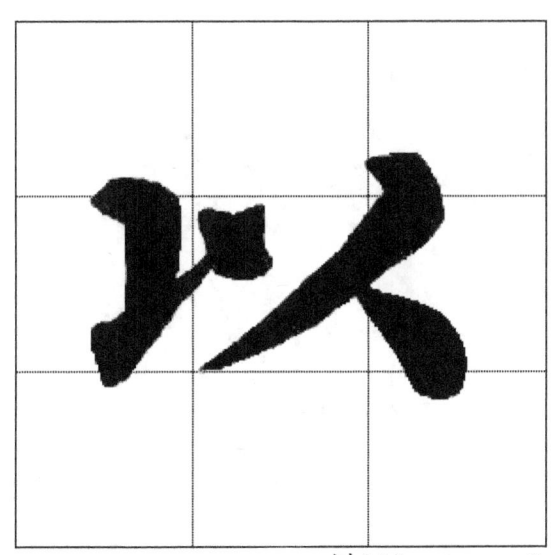

以/yǐ/by means of

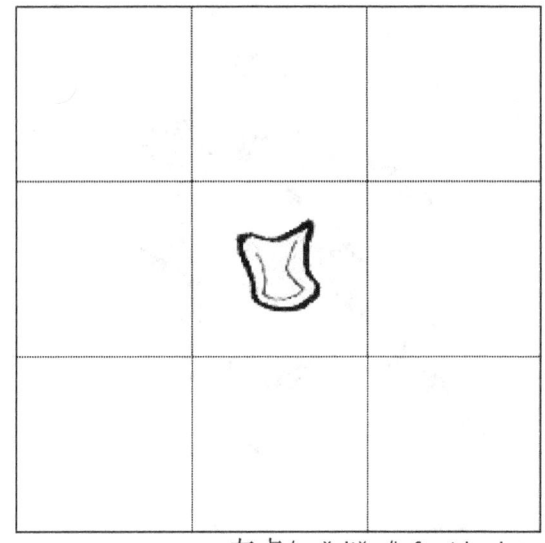

左点/zuǒdiǎn/left-side dot

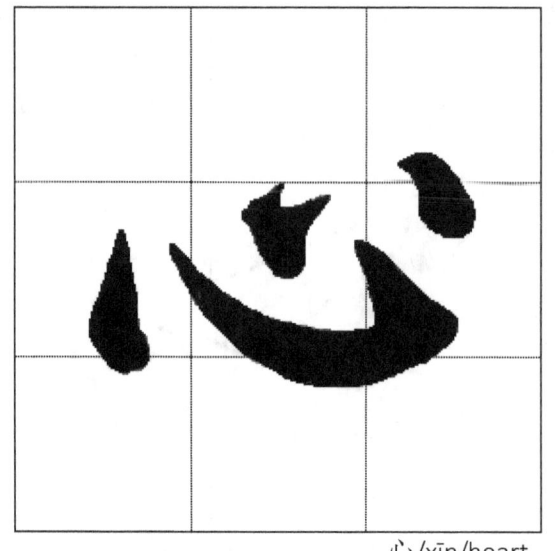

心/xīn/heart

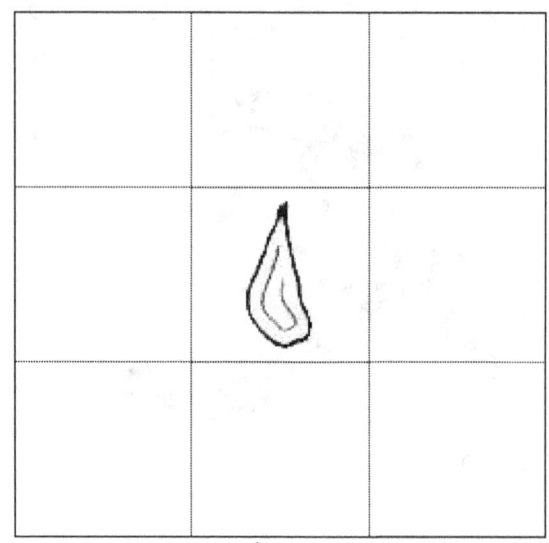

下点/xiàdiǎn/down-side dot

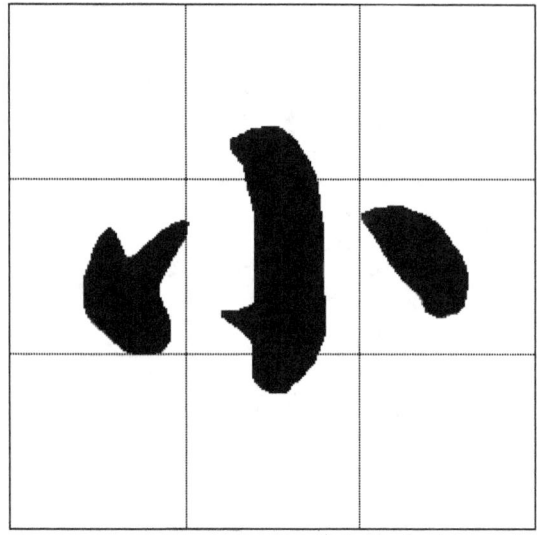

小/xiǎo/little, small

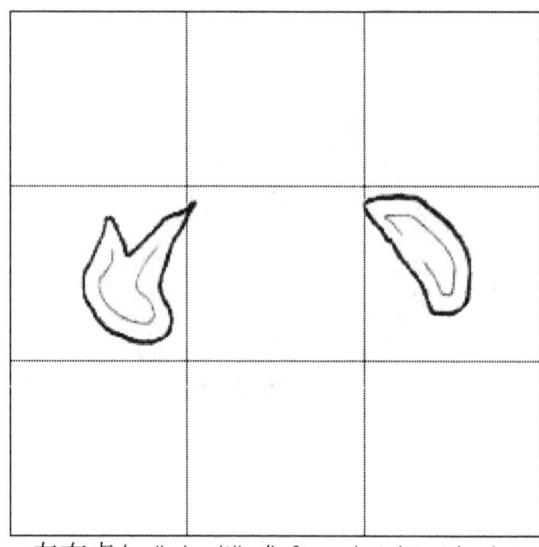

左右点/zuǒyòudiǎn/left-and-right-side dots

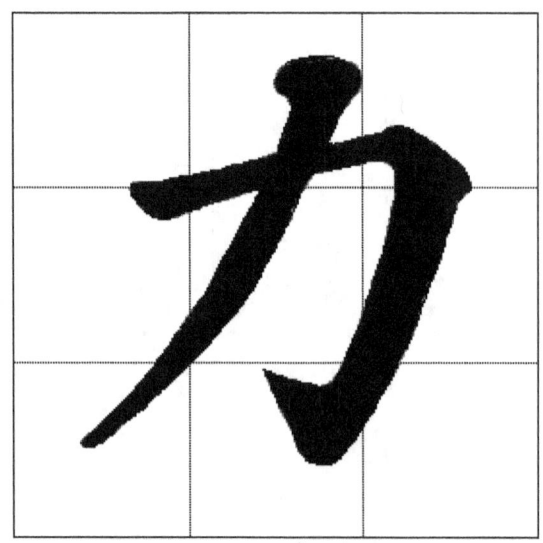

力/lì/strength, power

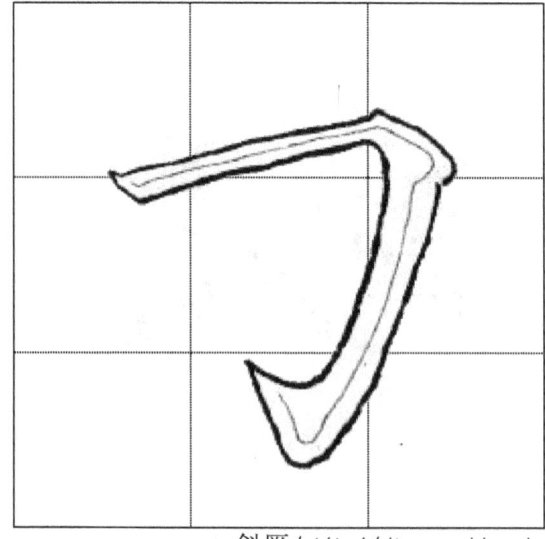

斜厥/xiéjué/diagonal hook

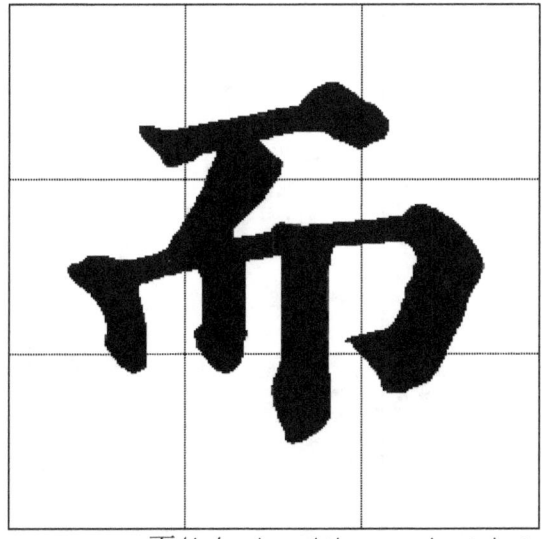

而/ér/and; and then; and yet; but

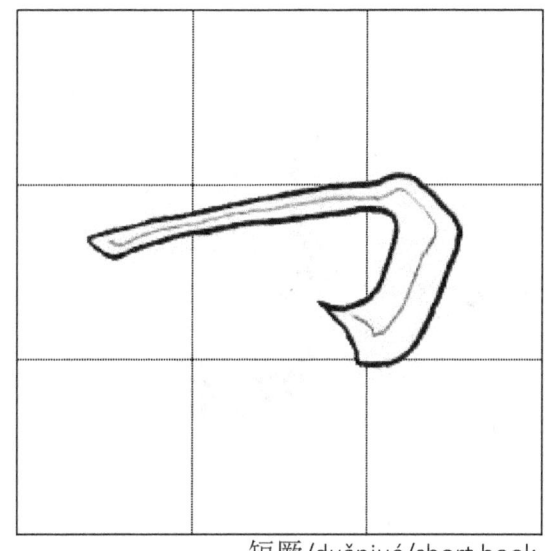

短厥/duǎnjué/short hook

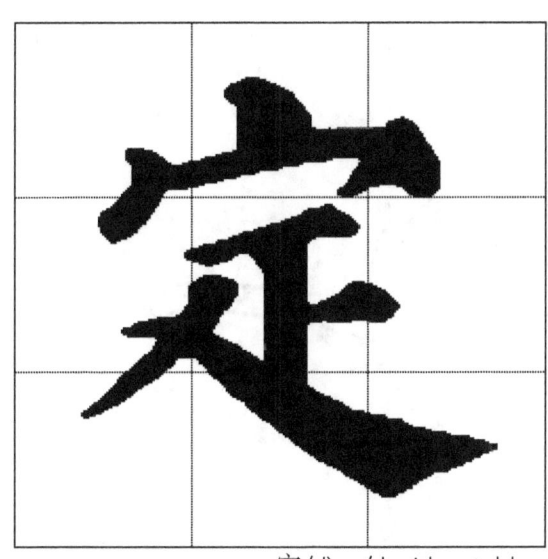

定/dìng/decide, stable

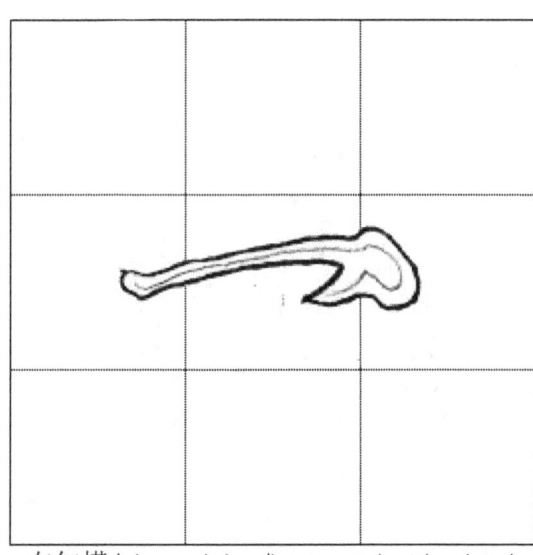

右勾横/yòugōuhéng/horizontal with a hook

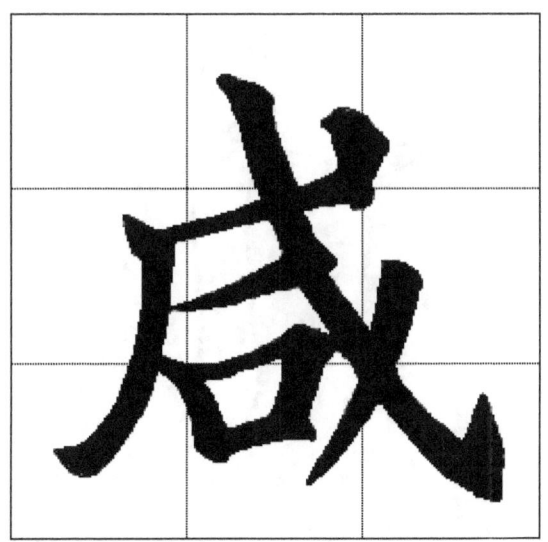

咸/xián/ all, together, completely

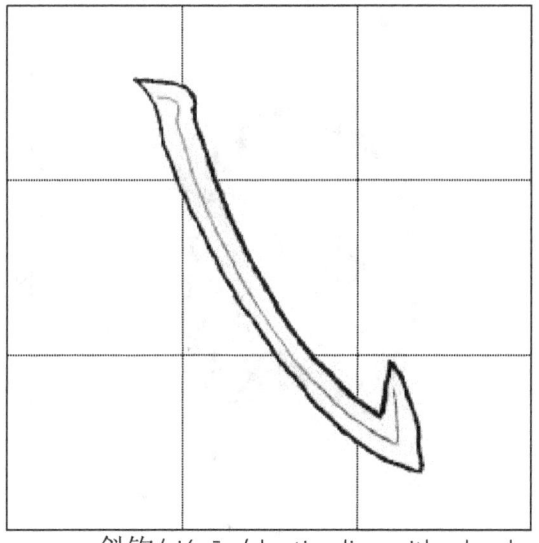

斜钩/xiégōu/slanting line with a hook

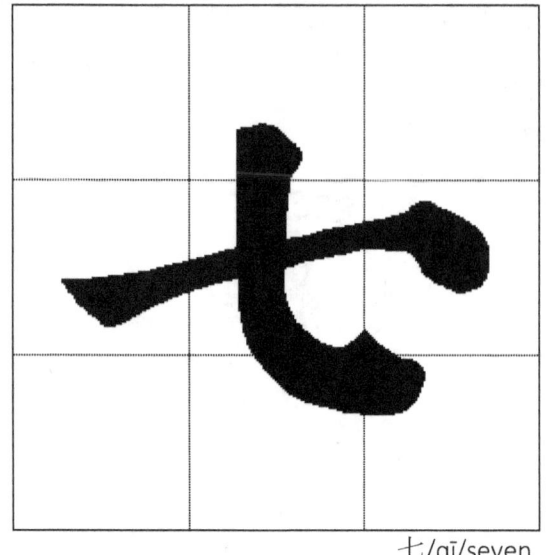

七/qī/seven

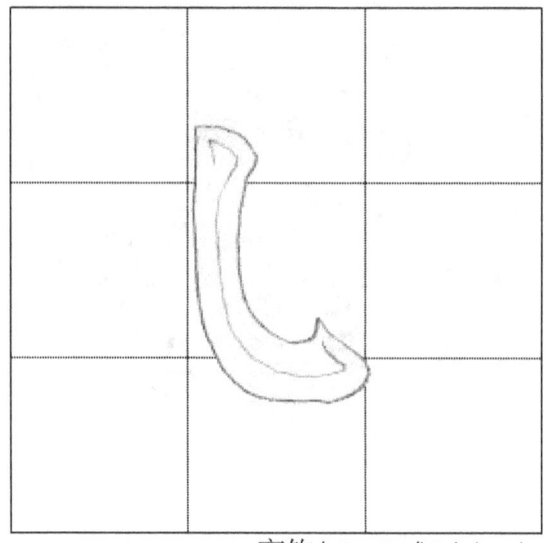

高钩/gāogōu/high hook

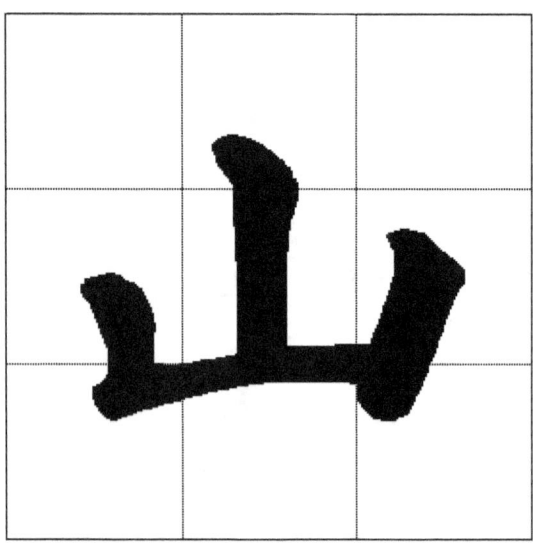

山/shān/mountain, hill

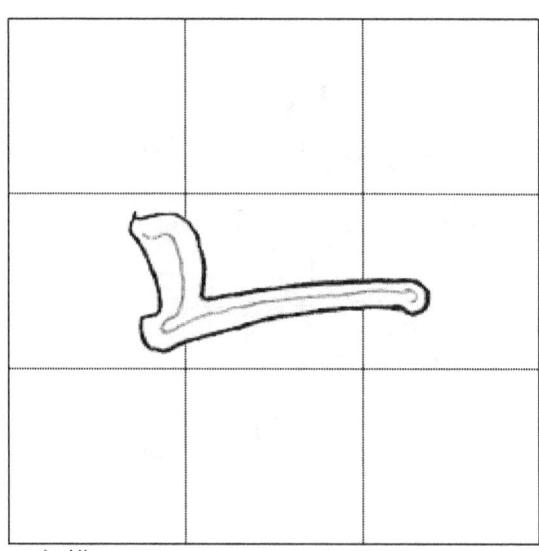

竖横/shùhéng/vertical turning to horizontal

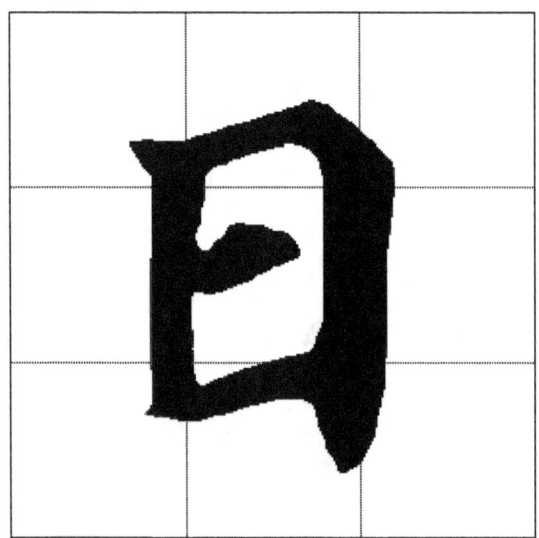

日/rì/ sun; day, daytime

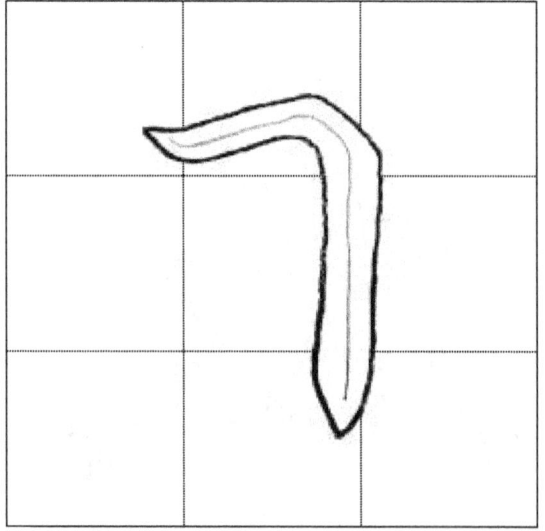

横竖/héngshù/horizontal turning to vertical

偏旁部首集字
Characters by Radicals

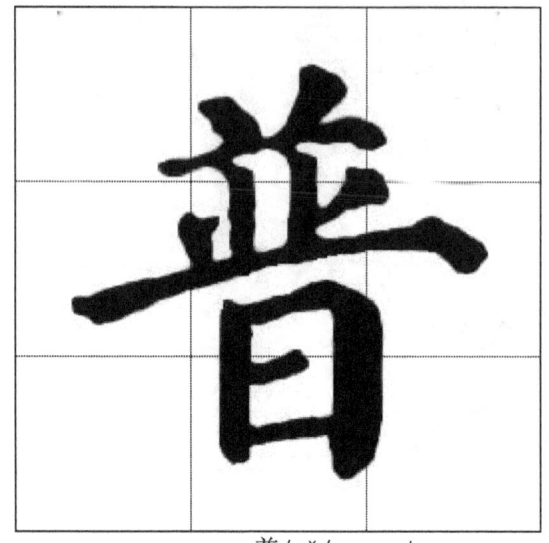

普/pǔ/general, common

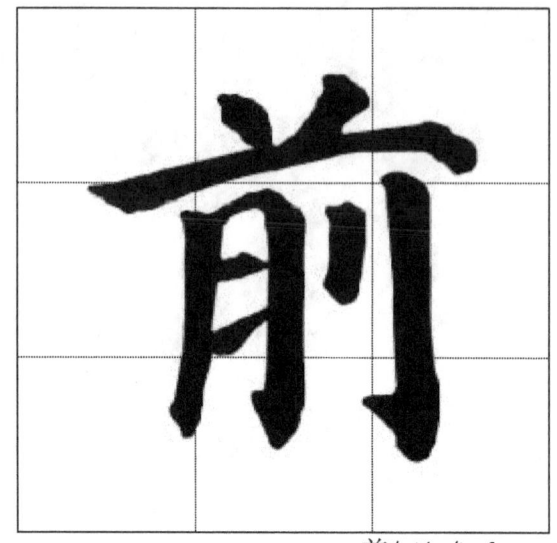

前/qián/in front

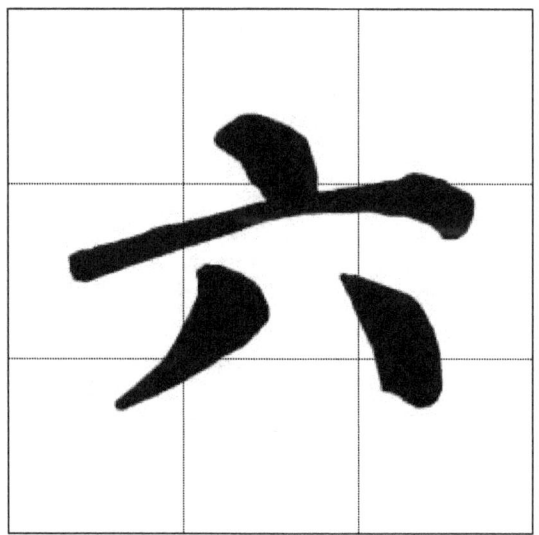

六/liù/six

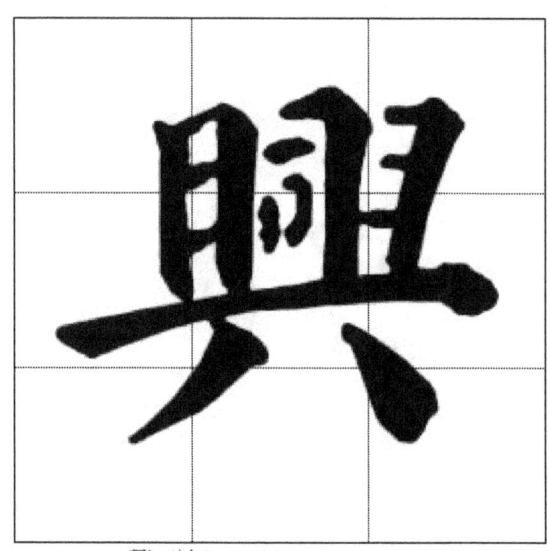

興=兴/xīng/thrive, prosper, flourish

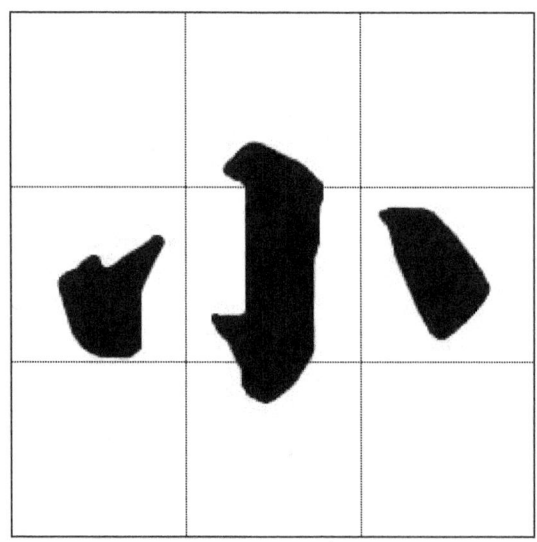

小/xiǎo/little, small

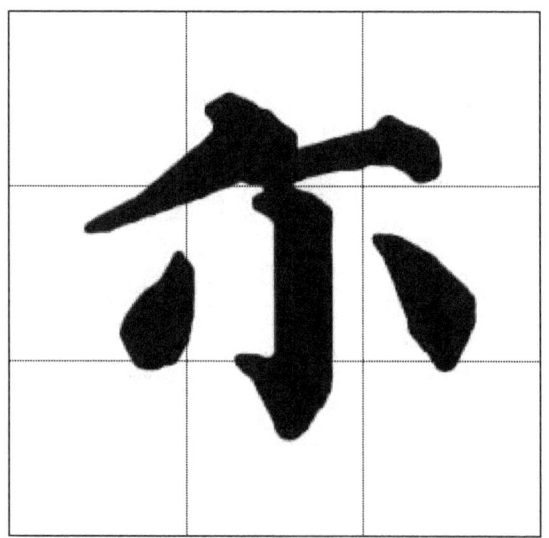

尔/ěr/you; that, those; final particle

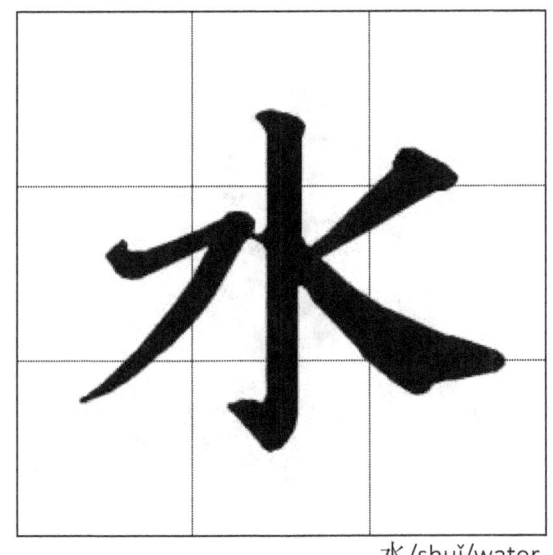

水/shuǐ/water

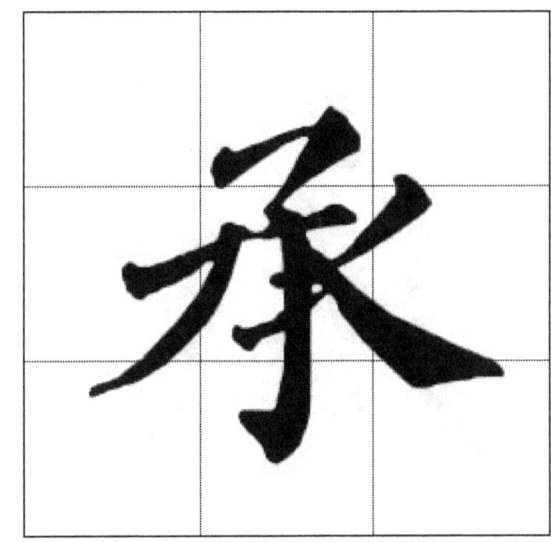

承/chéng/bear, undertake

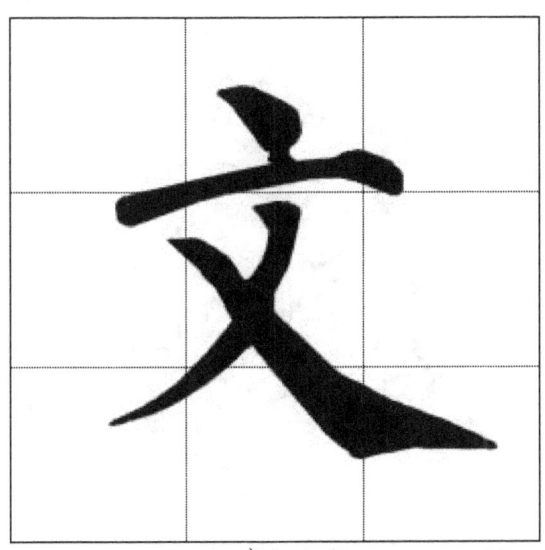

文/wén/literature, writing

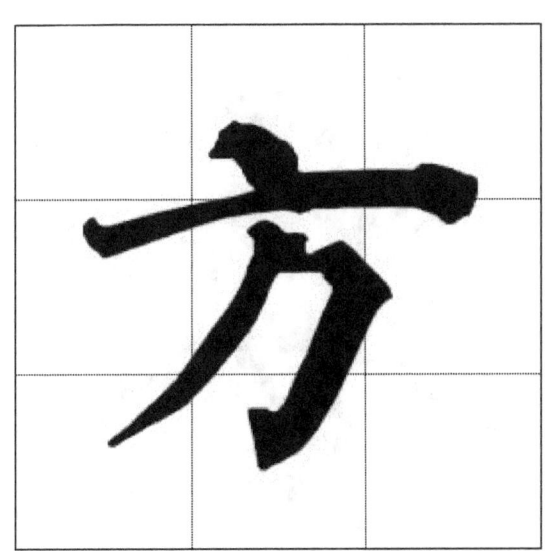

方/fāng/a square, rectangle

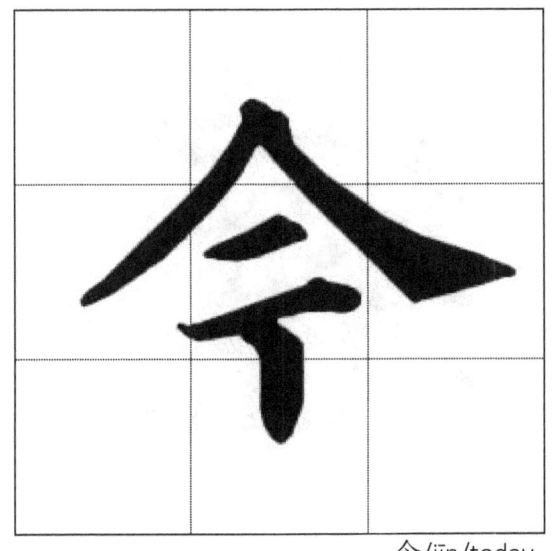

今/jīn/today

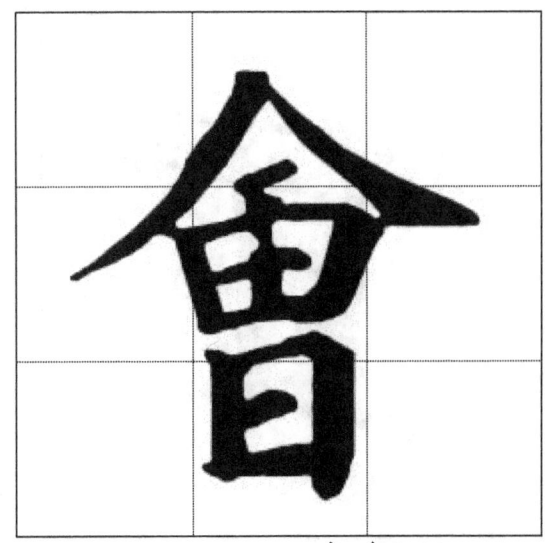

會=会/huì/meeting

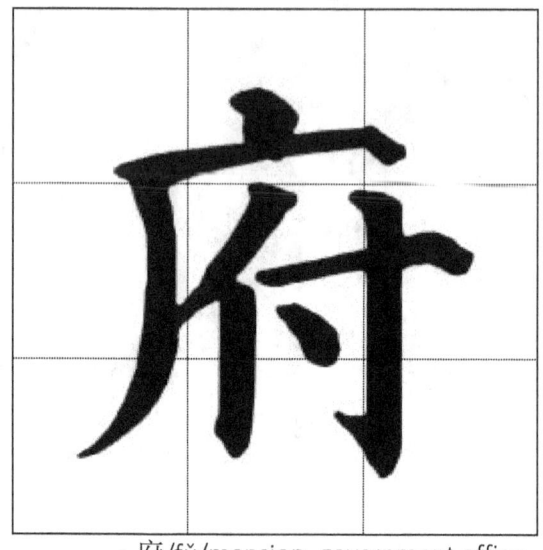

府/fǔ/mansion, government office

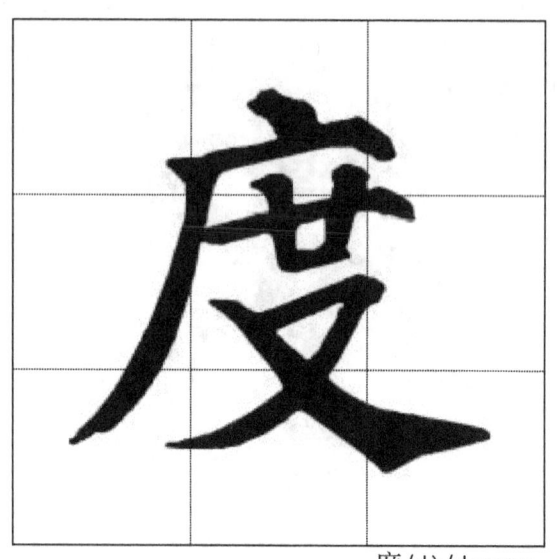

度/dù/degree

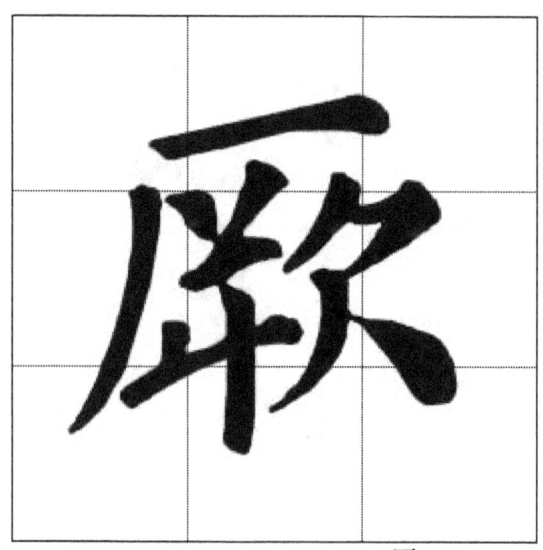

厥/jué/faint

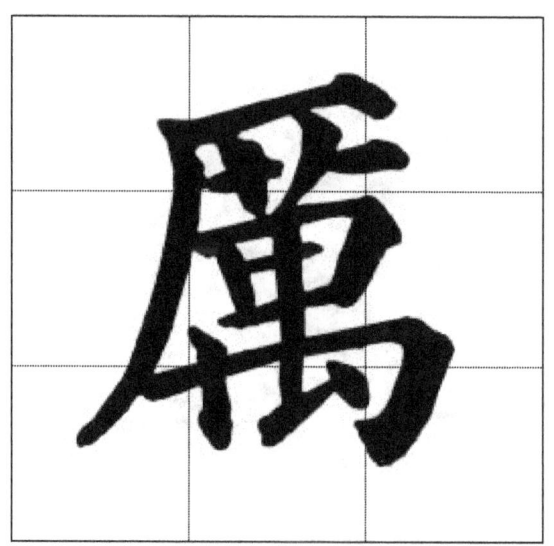

厲=厉/lì/severe, strict

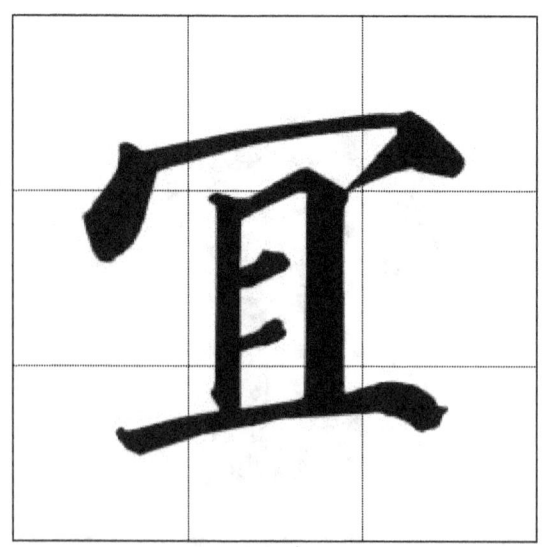

宐=宜/yí/suitable, proper

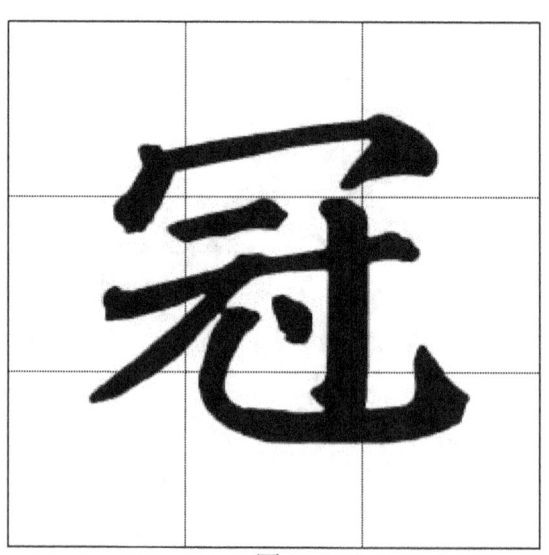

冠/guàn/coronal, crown

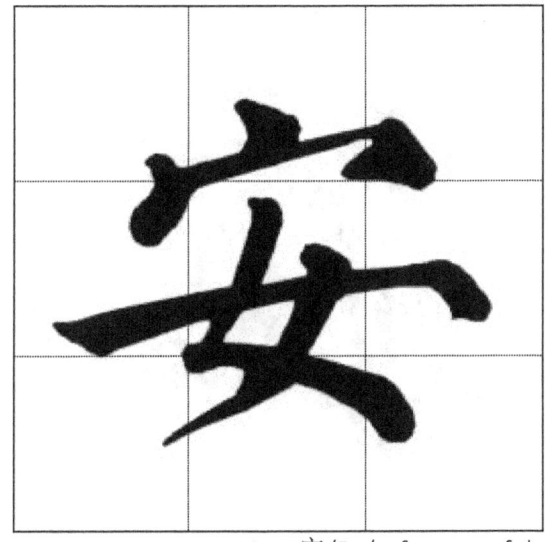
安/ān/safe, peaceful

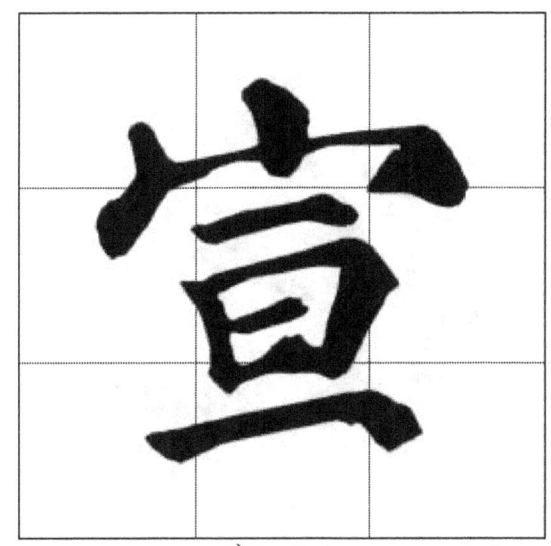
宣/xuān/announce, declare

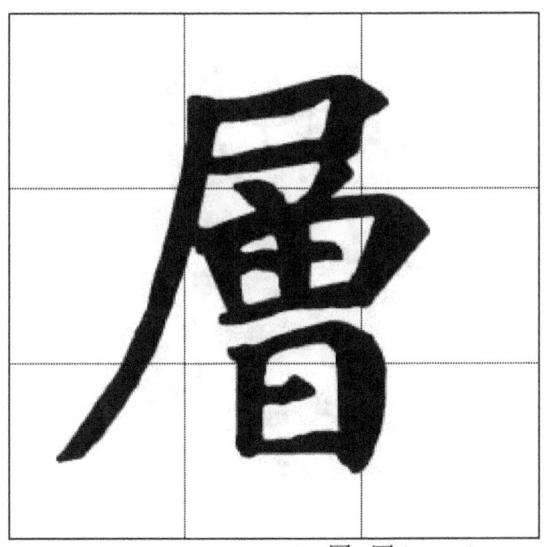
層=层/céng/story

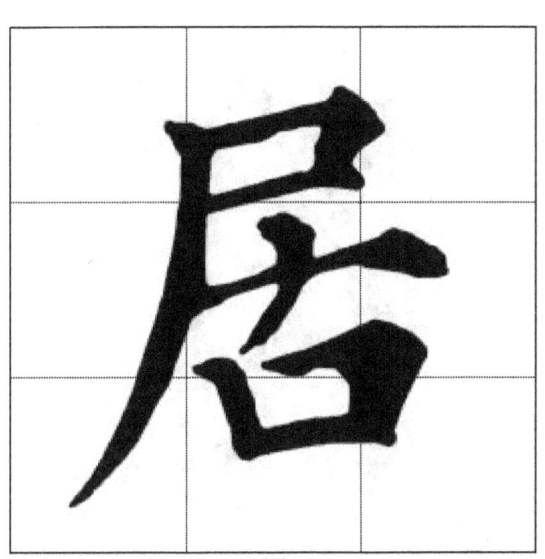
居/jū/live, dwell, reside

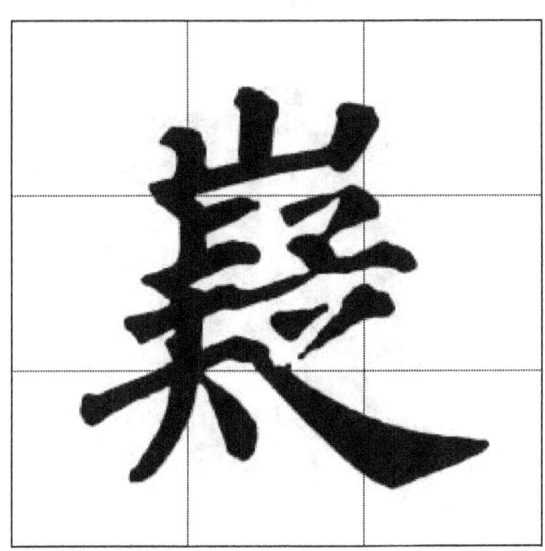
嶷/yí/a range of mountains in Hunan province

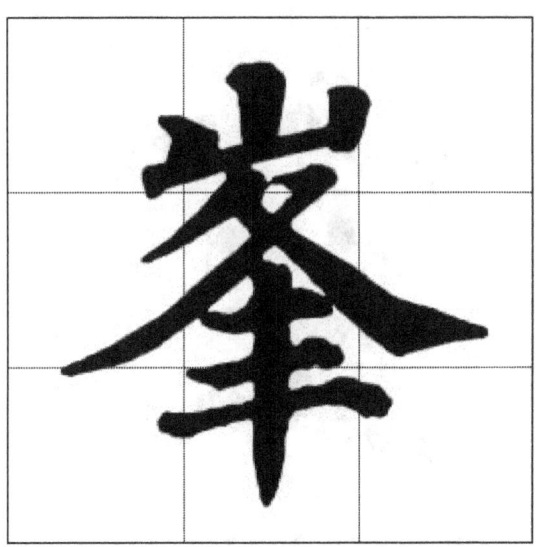
峯=峰/fēng/peak, summit

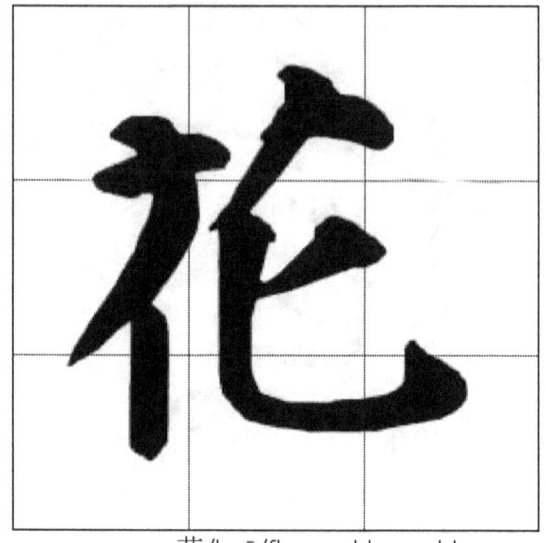

花/huā/flower, bloom, blossom

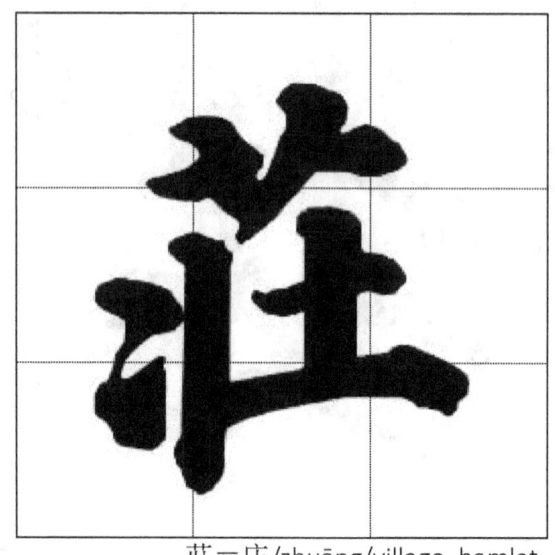

莊＝庄/zhuāng/village, hamlet

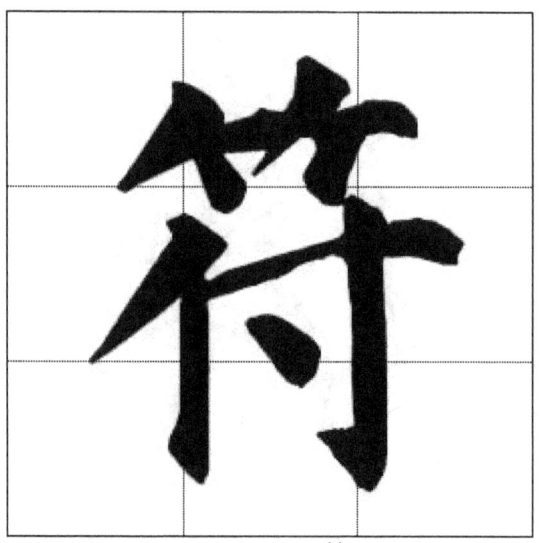

符/fú/symbol, tag

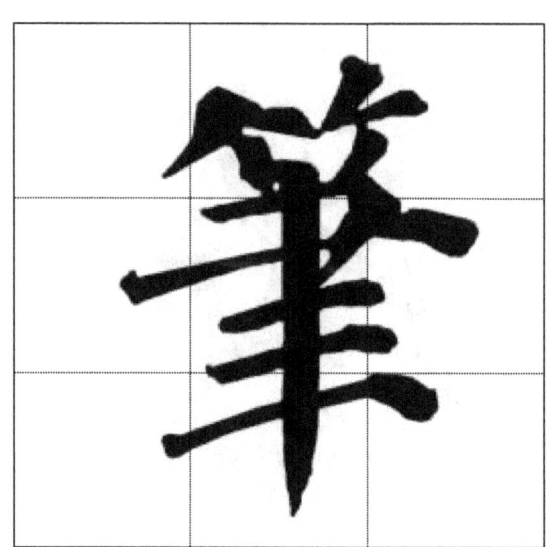

筆＝笔/bǐ/pen, writing brush

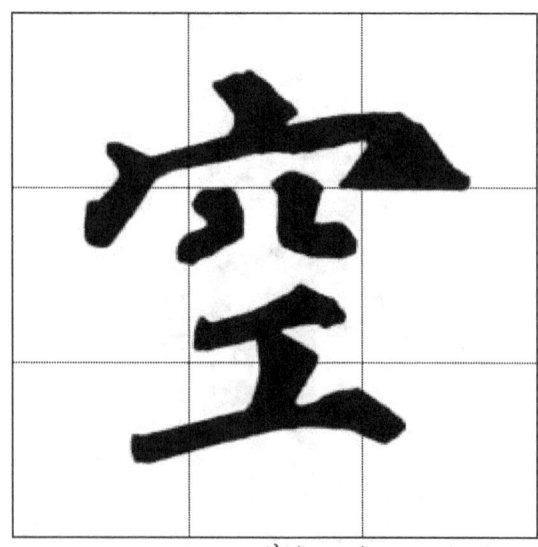

空/kōng/empty, hollow

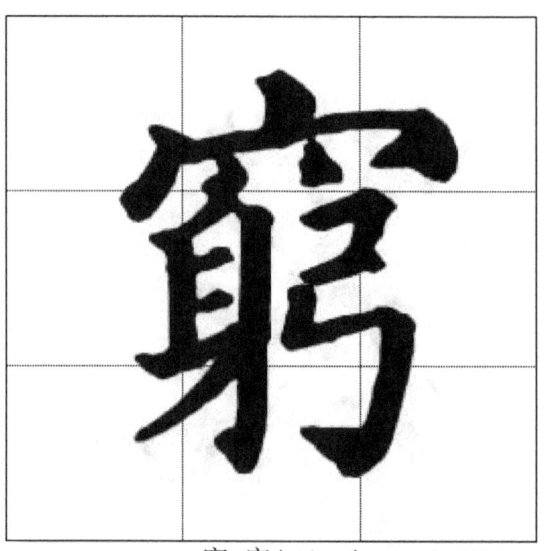

窮＝穷/qióng/poor, destitute

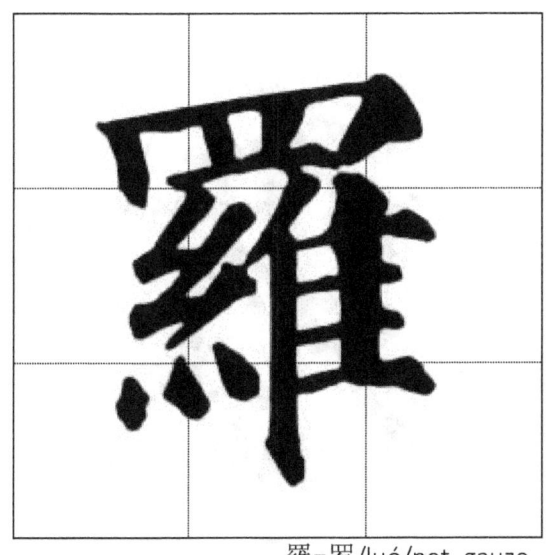

羅=罗/luó/net, gauze

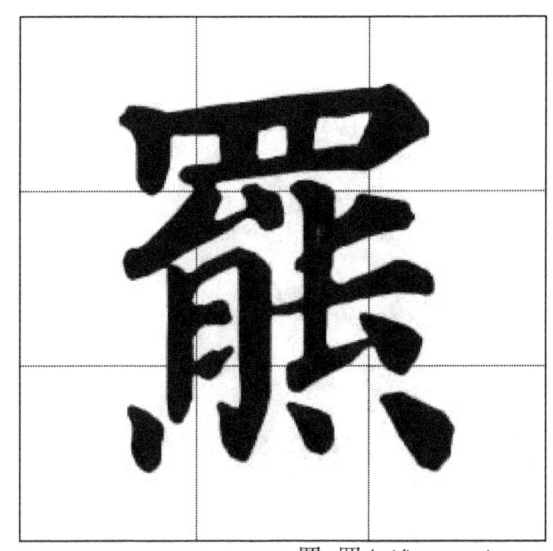

羆=罴/pí/brown bear

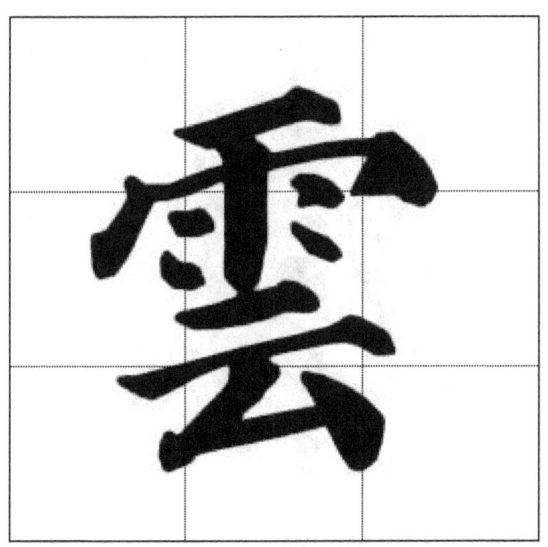

雲=云/yún/cloud, say

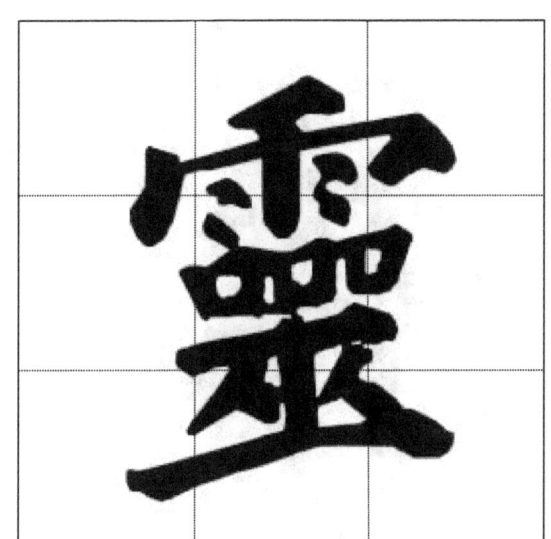

靈=灵/líng/soul, spirit

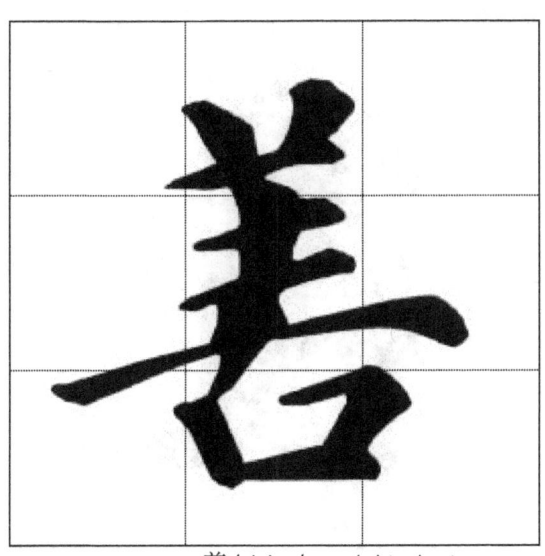

善/shàn/good, kind, virtuous

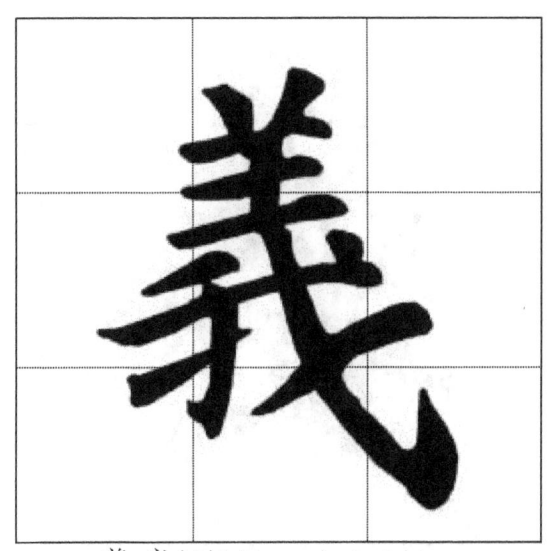

義=义/yì/right conduct, righteousness

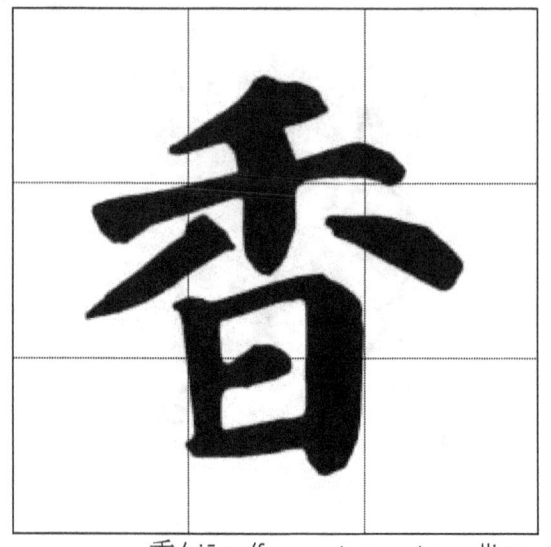

香/xiāng/fragrant, sweet smelling

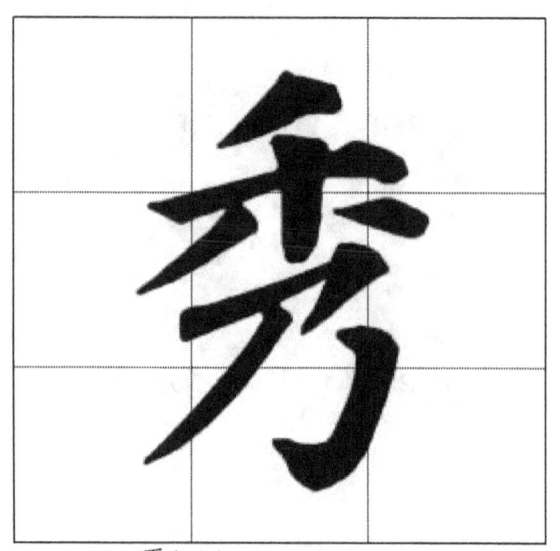

秀/xiù/beautiful, elegant, excellent

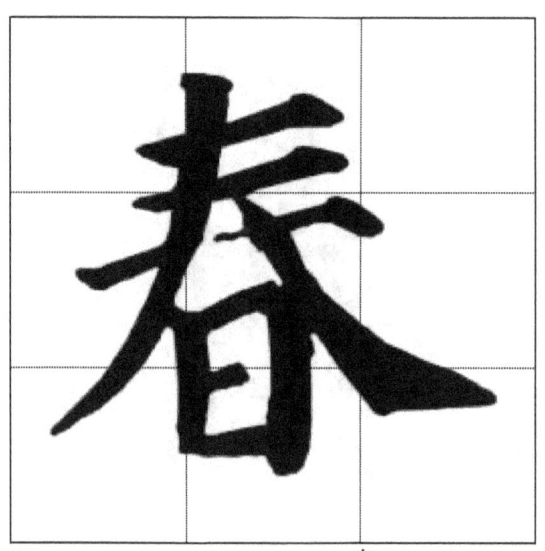

春/chūn/spring

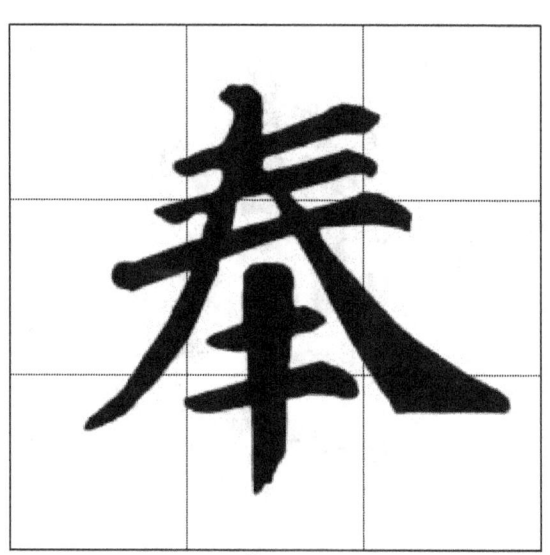

奉/fèng/give with respect

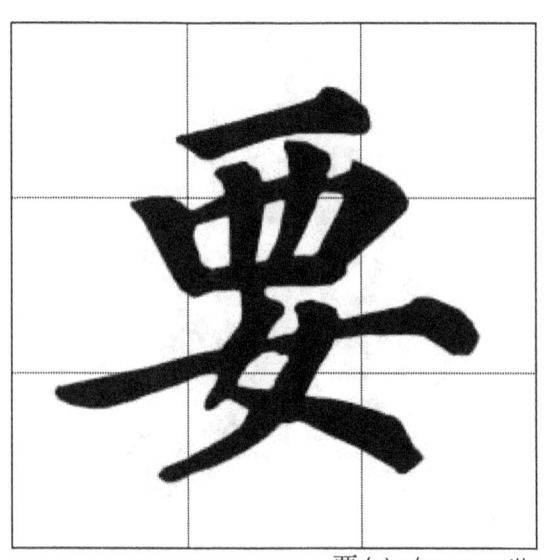

要/yào/want, will

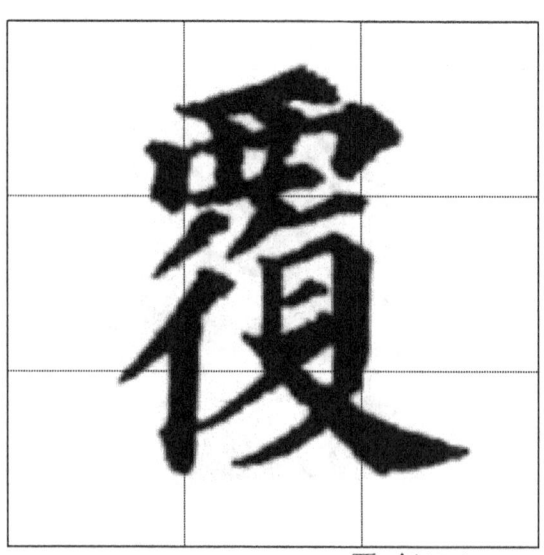

覆=复/fù/cover

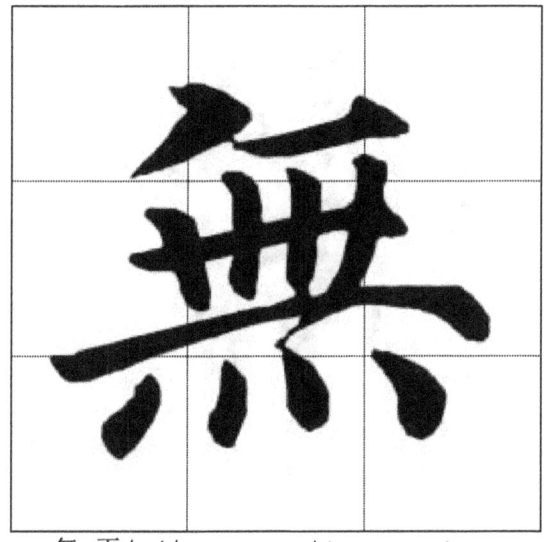

無=无/wú/no, not, nothing, nonexistence

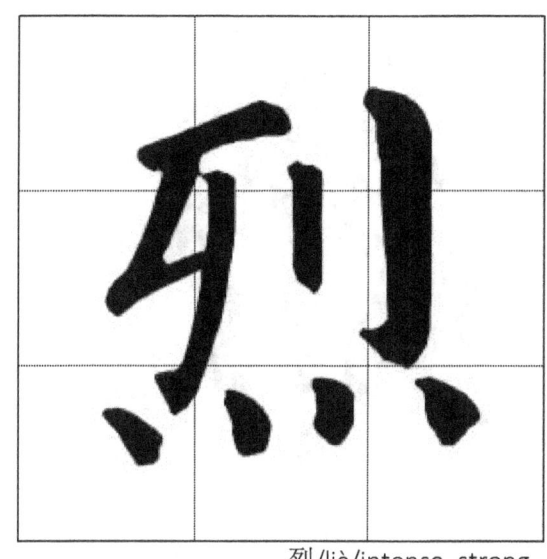

烈/liè/intense, strong

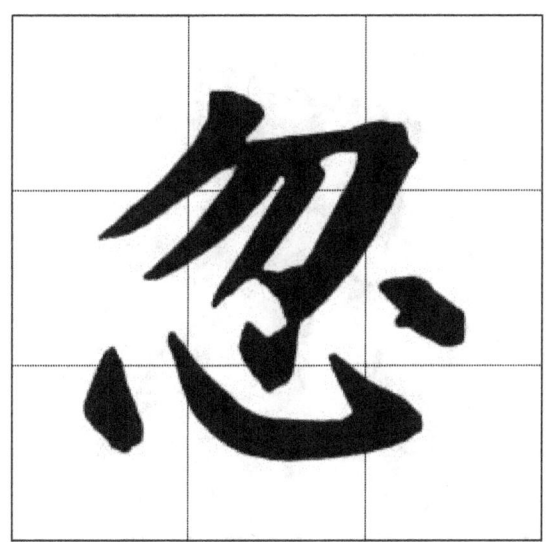

忽/hū/suddenly, abruptly

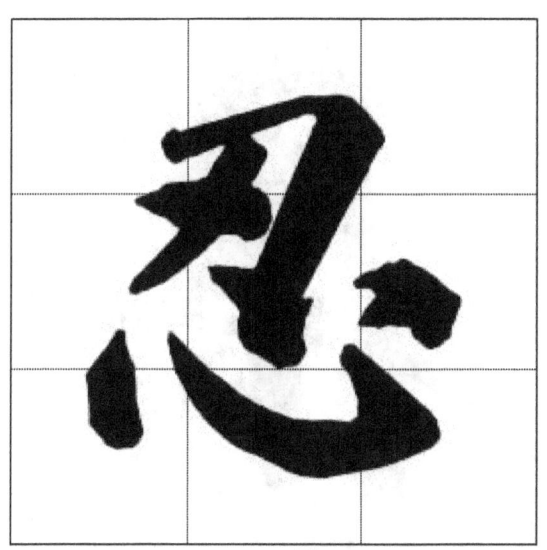

忍/rěn/bear, endure

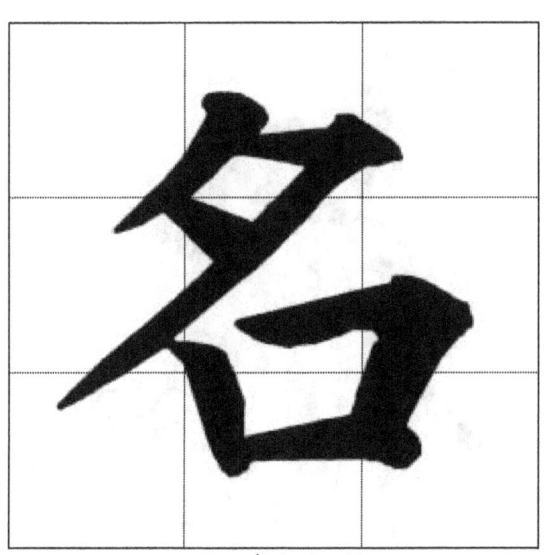

名/míng/first name, title

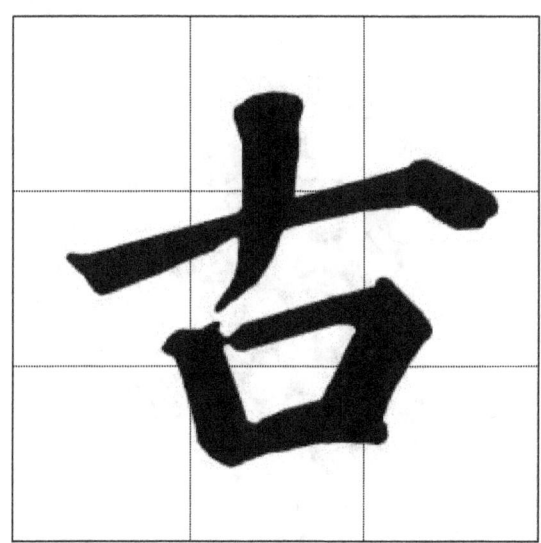

古/gǔ/old, ancient

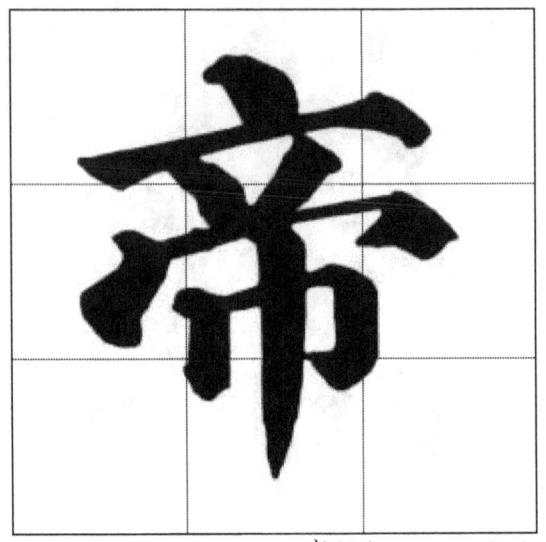

帝/dì/emperor, God

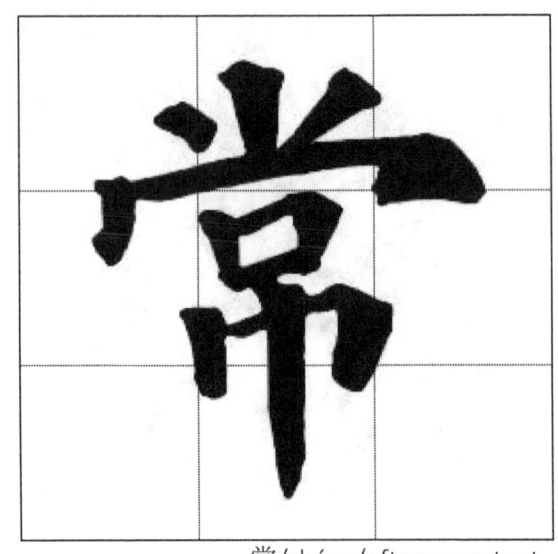

常/cháng/often, constant

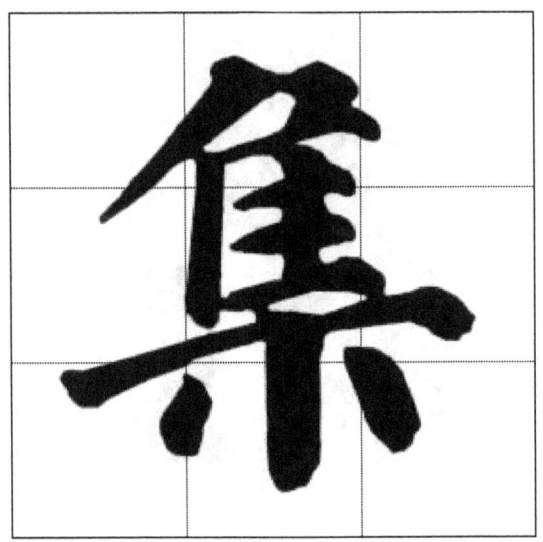

集/jí/gather, collect

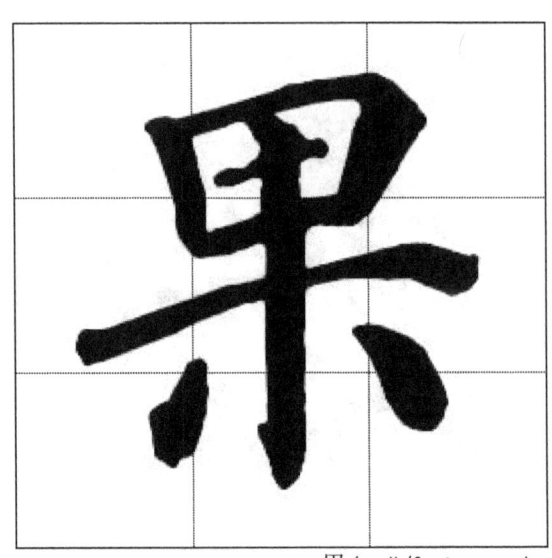

果/guǒ/fruit, result

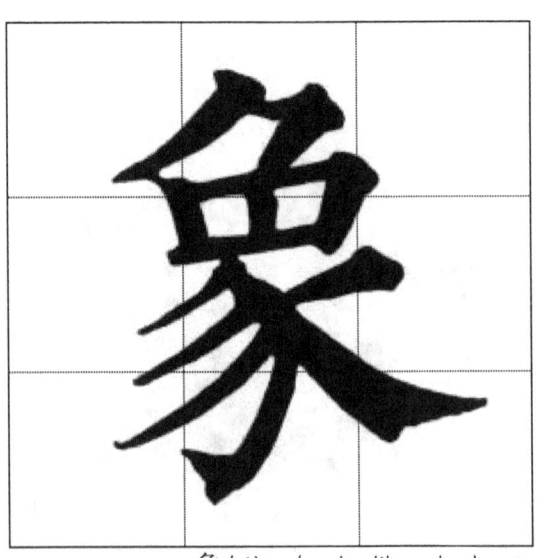

象/xiàng/as, be like, elephant

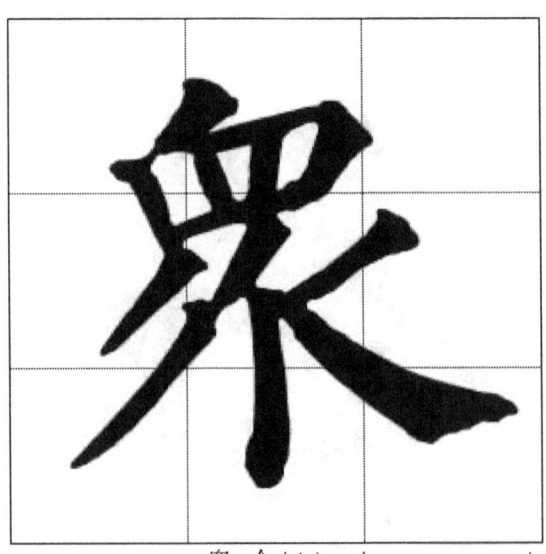

眾=众/zhòng/masses, crowd

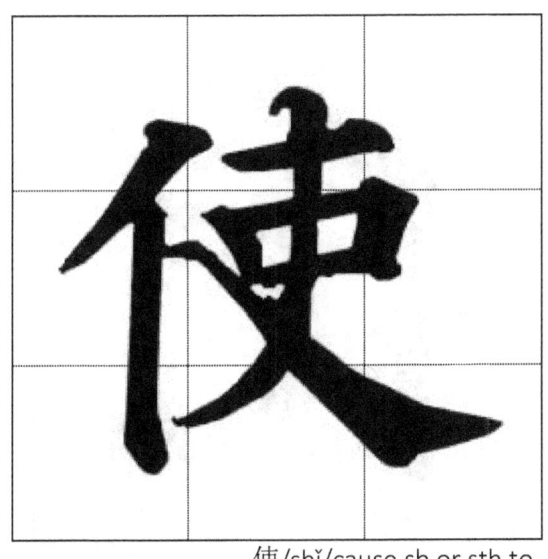

使/shǐ/cause sb or sth to

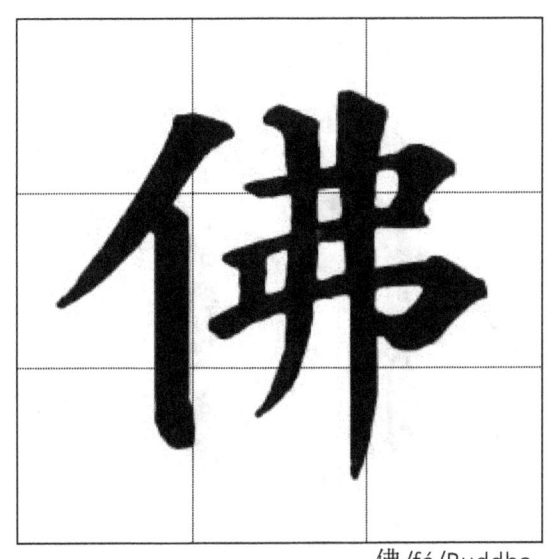

佛/fó/Buddha

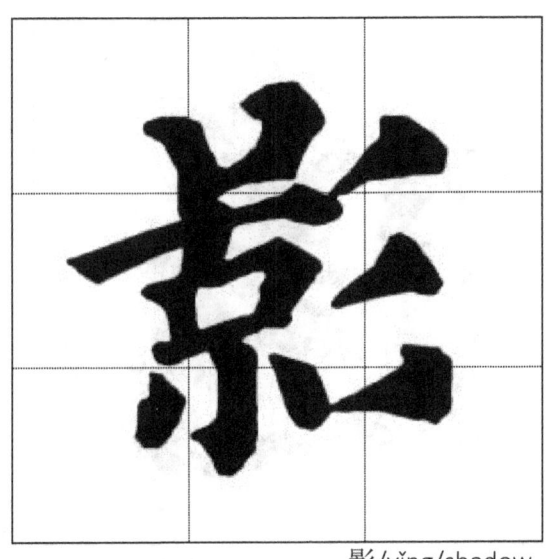

影/yǐng/shadow

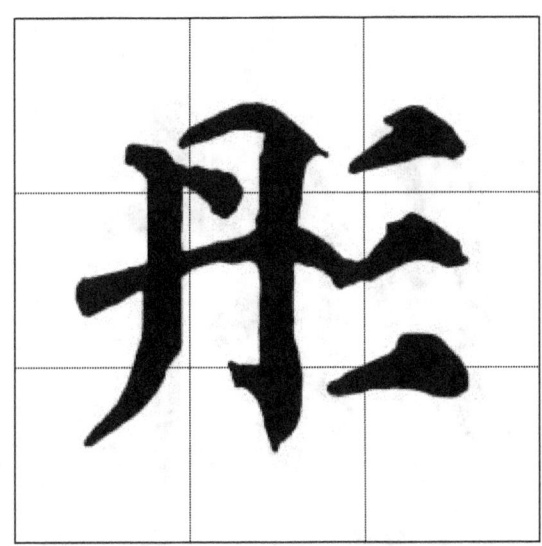

彤/tóng/red, vermilion

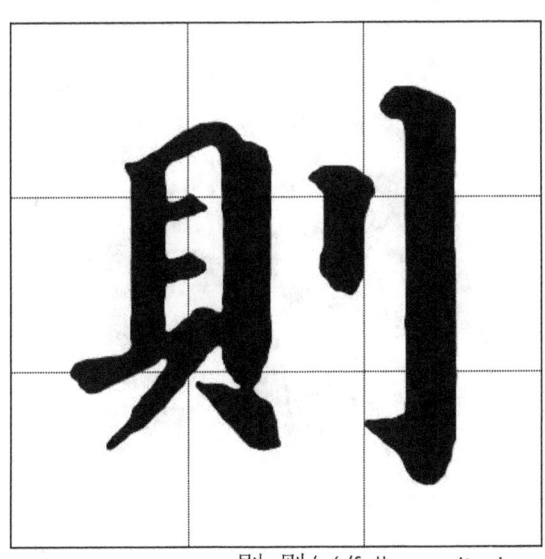

則=则/zé/follow, criterion

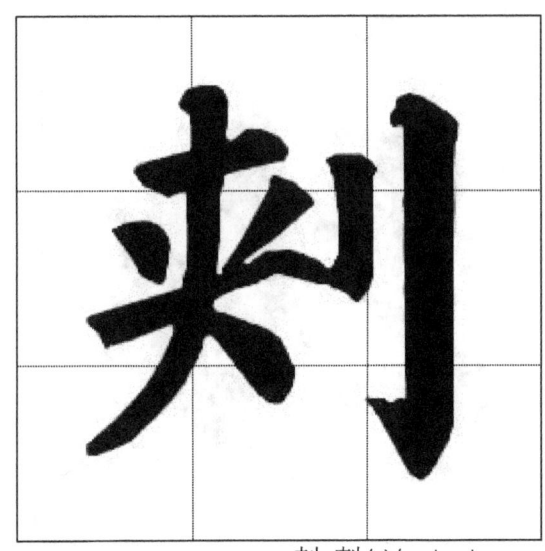

剌=剌/cì/stab, thrust

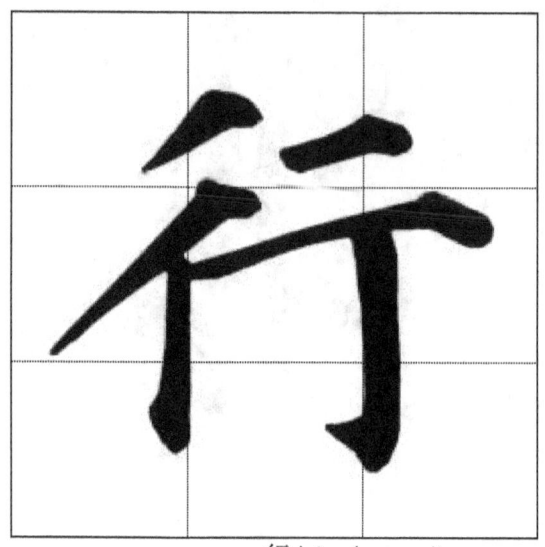

行/xíng/go, walk, move

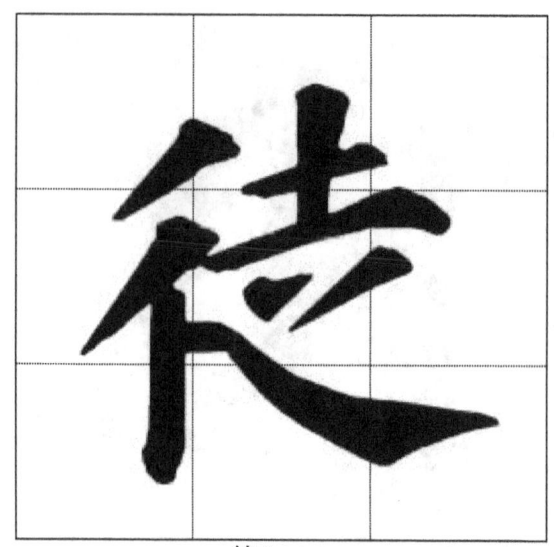

徒/tú/apprentice, disciple

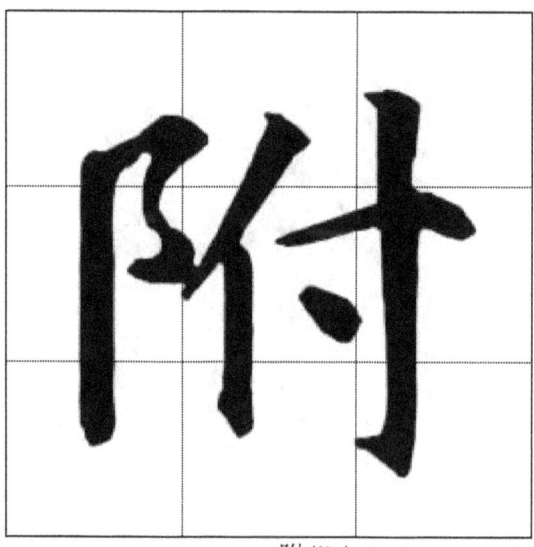

附/fù/attach, append

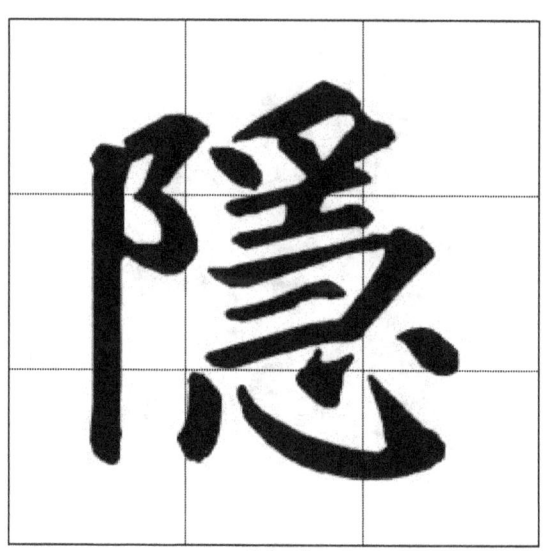

隱=隐/yǐn/ hide, conceal

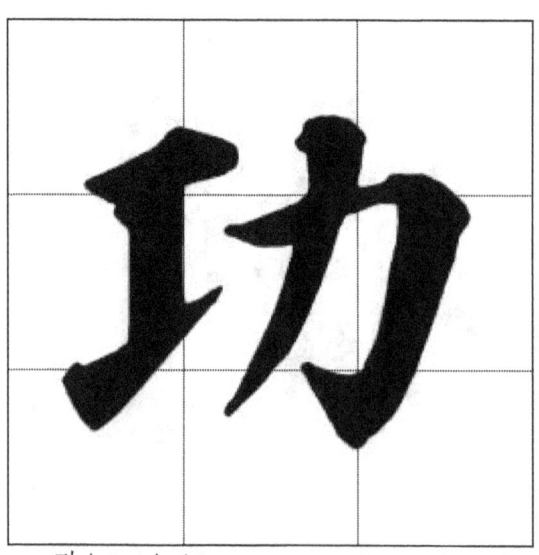

功/gōng/achievement, merit, good result

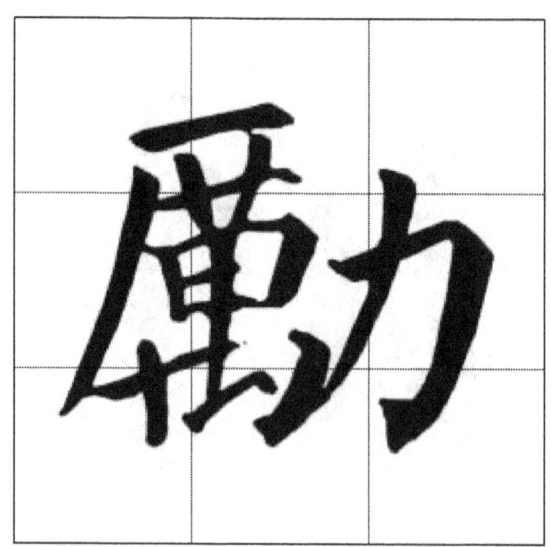

勵=励/lì/encourage

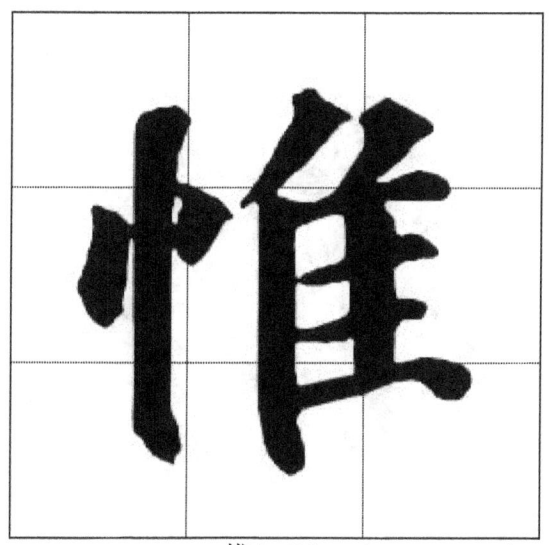

惟/wéi/but, however, only

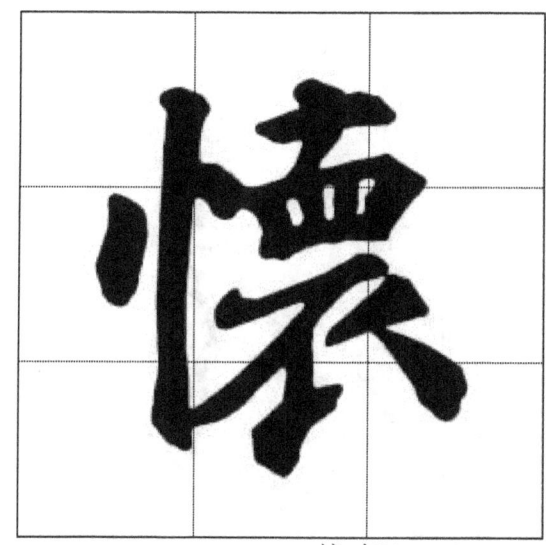

懷=怀/huái/bosom

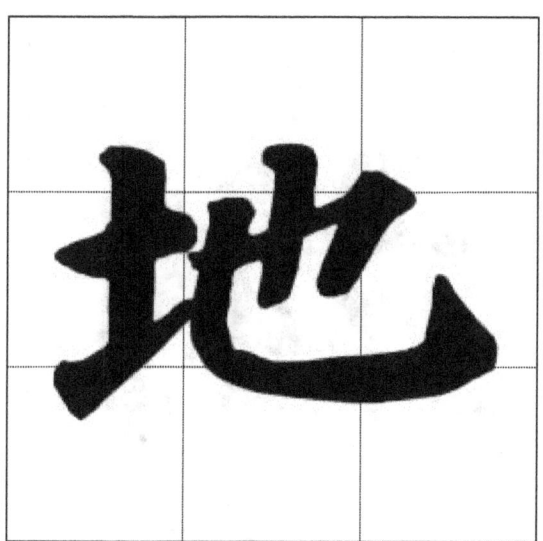

地/dì/earth, soil, ground

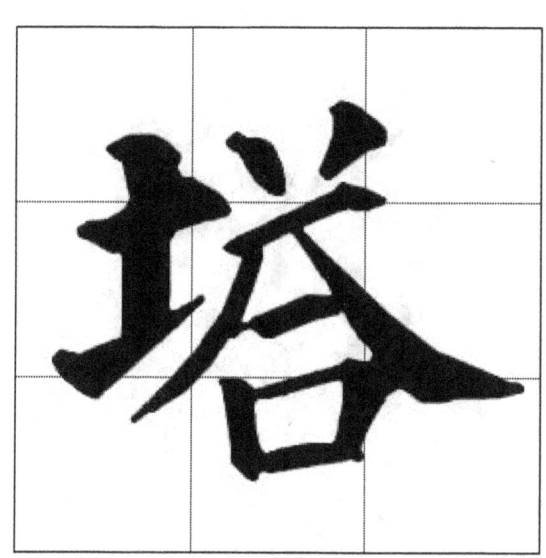

塔/tǎ/pagoda, tower

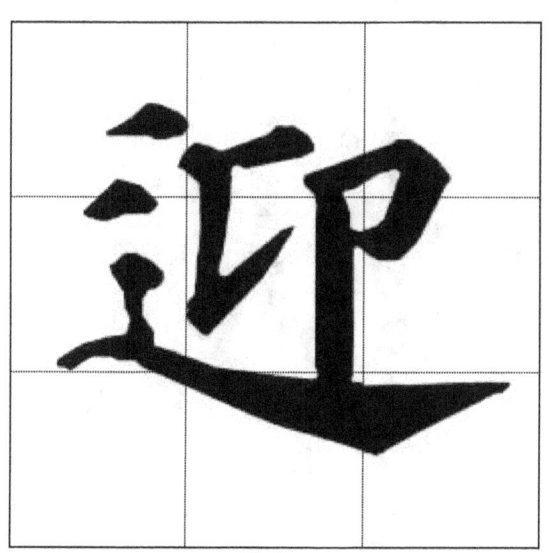

迎/yíng/receive, welcome

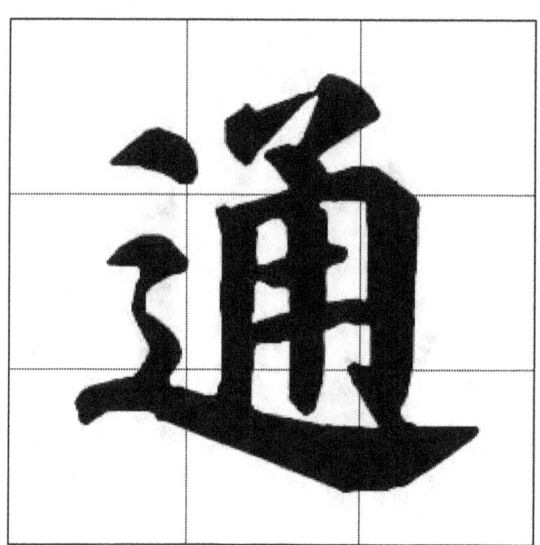

通/tōng/pass through

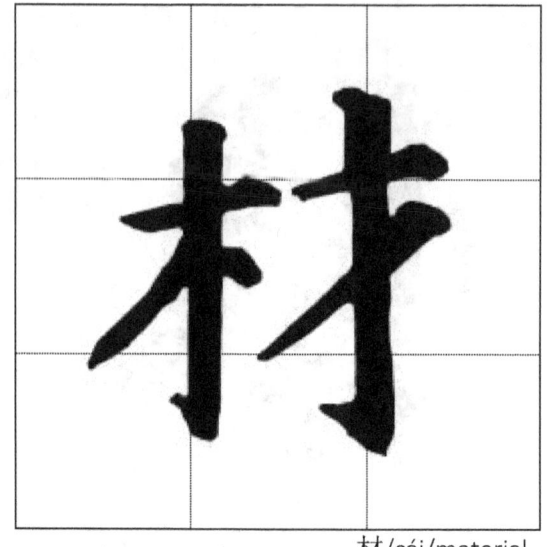

材/cái/material

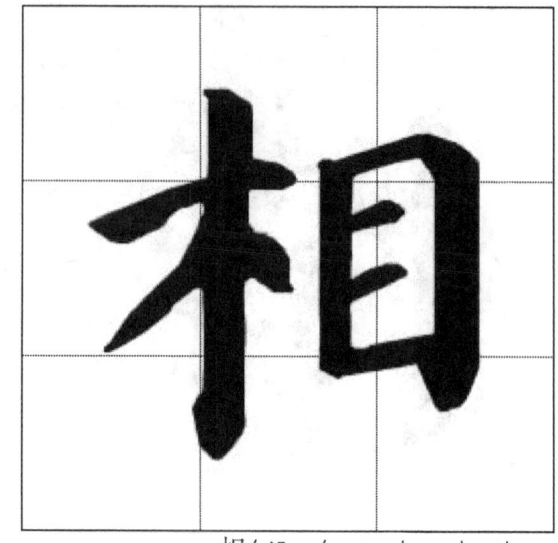

相/xiāng/mutual, each other

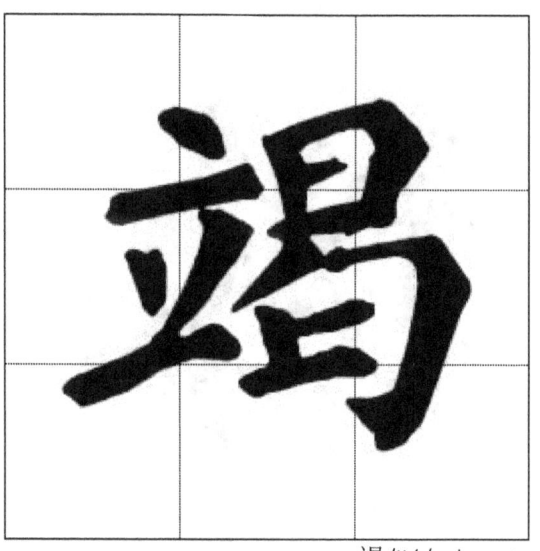

竭/jié/exhaust

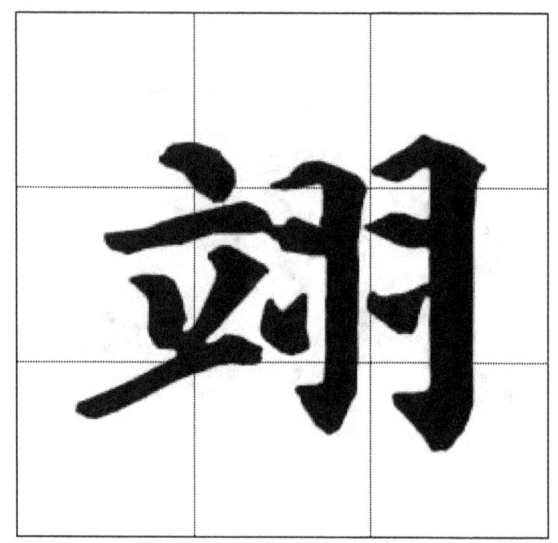

翊/yì/assist, help

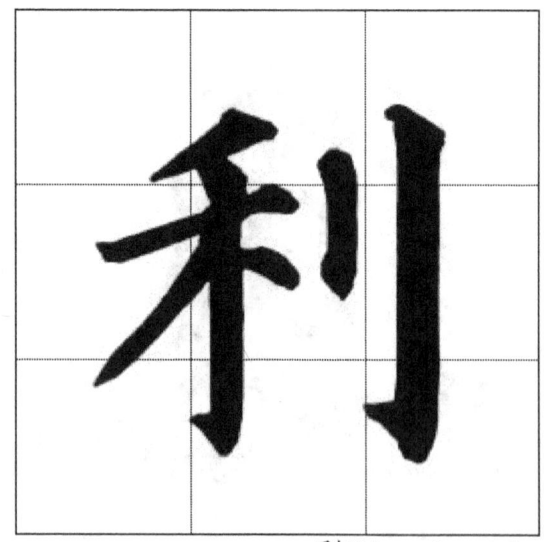

利/lì/benefit, profit

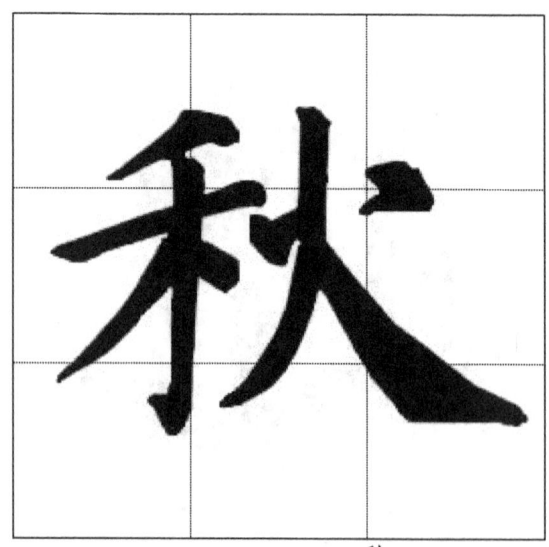

秋/qiū/autumn

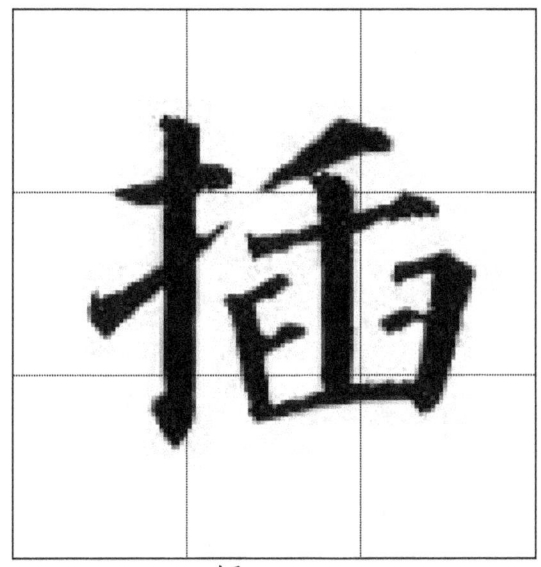

插/chā/ insert, stick into

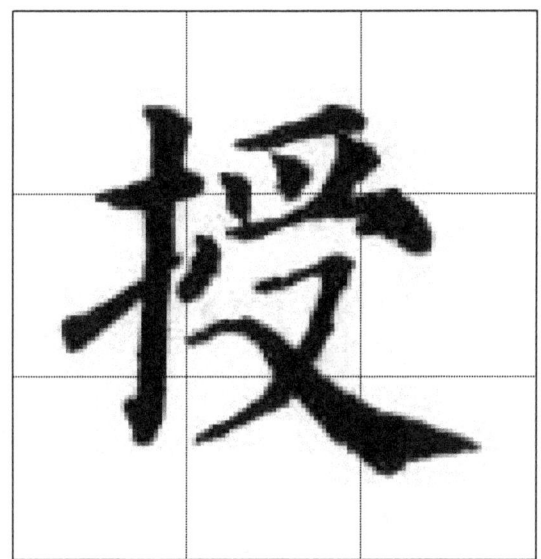

授/shòu/give to; teach

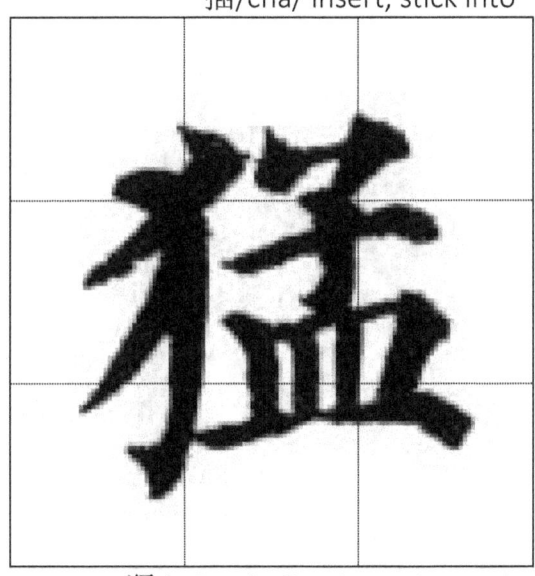

猛/měng/violently, with a rush

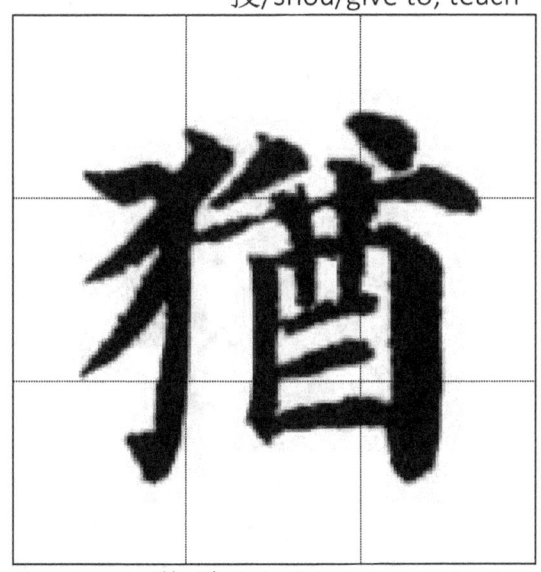

猶=犹/yóu/like, as, similar to

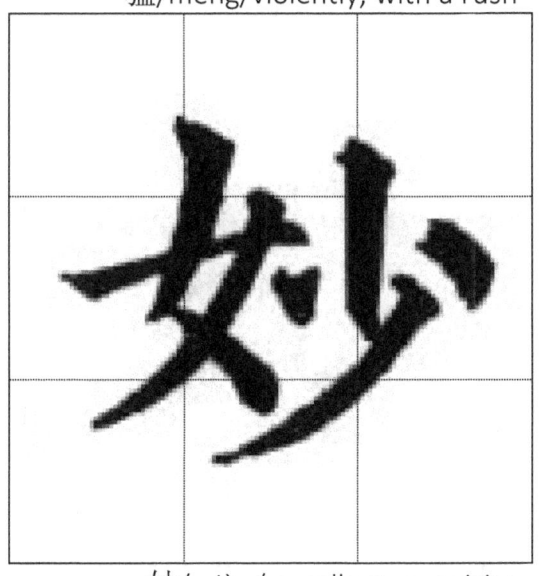

妙/miào/ excellent, exquisite

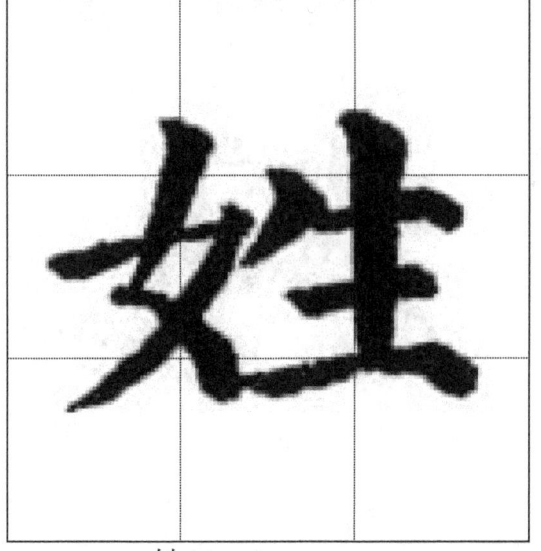

姓/xìng/last name, surname

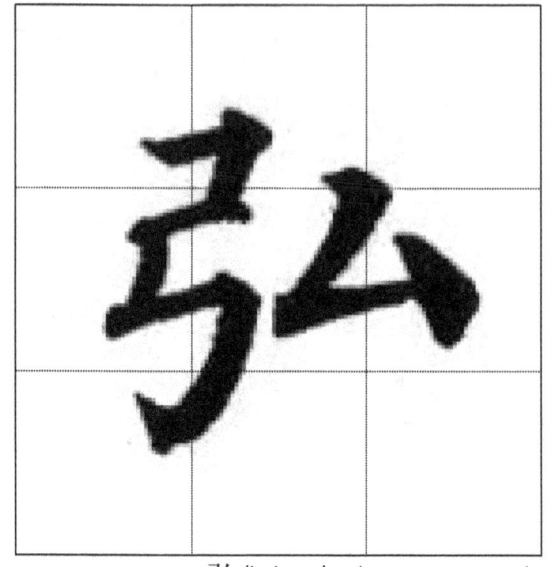

弘/hóng/enlarge, expand

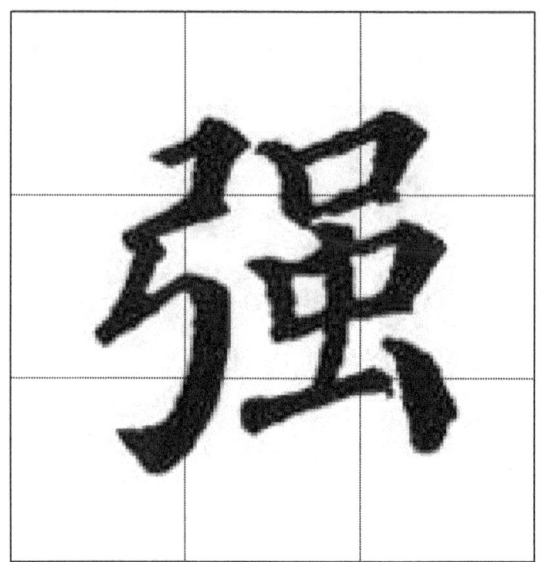

强/qiáng strong, powerful, energetic

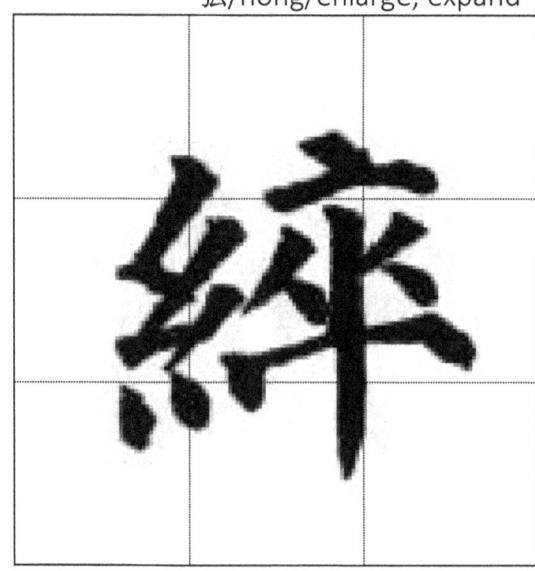

綷/cuì/five-color silk

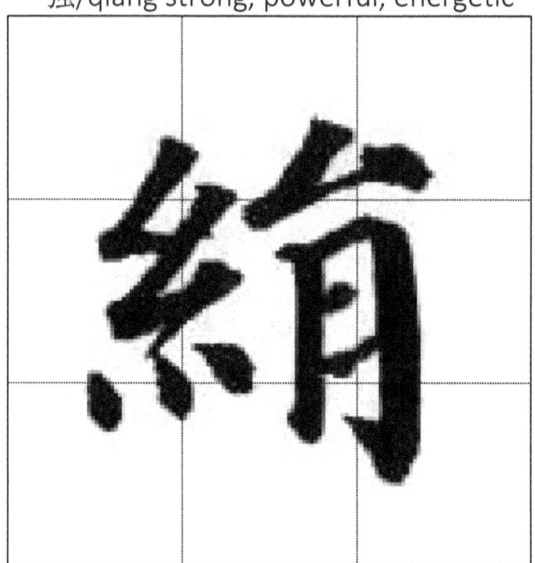

絹=绢/juàn/kind of silk

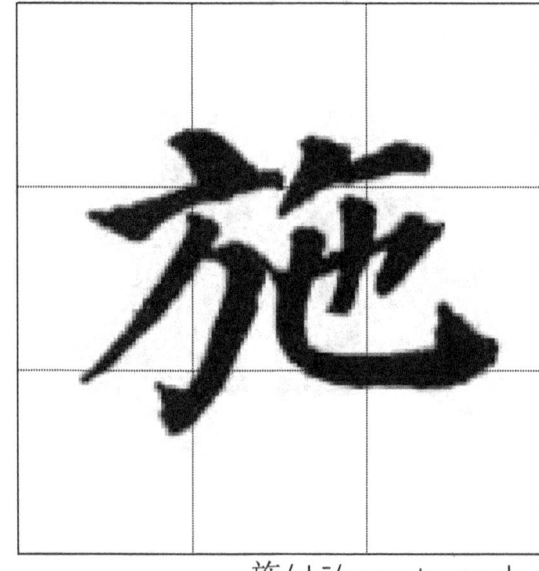

施/shī/execute, apply

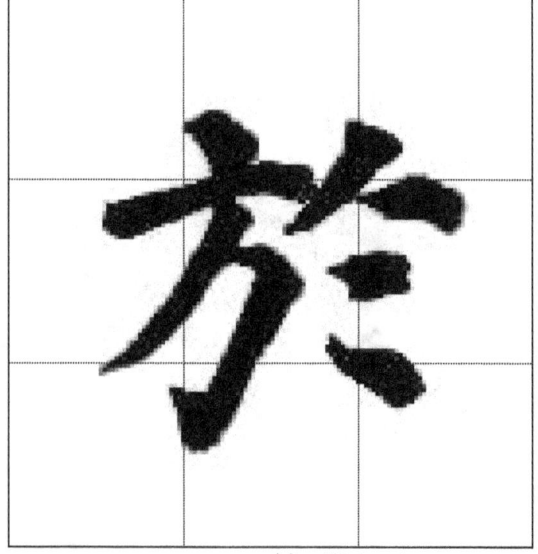

於=于/yú/ in, on, at

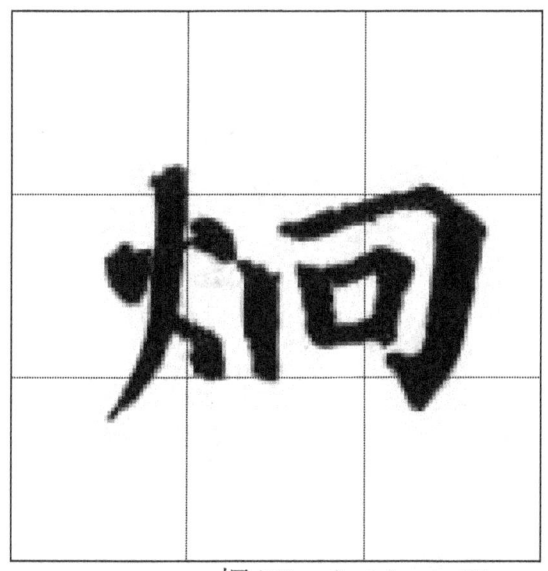

炯/jiǒng/bright, brilliant

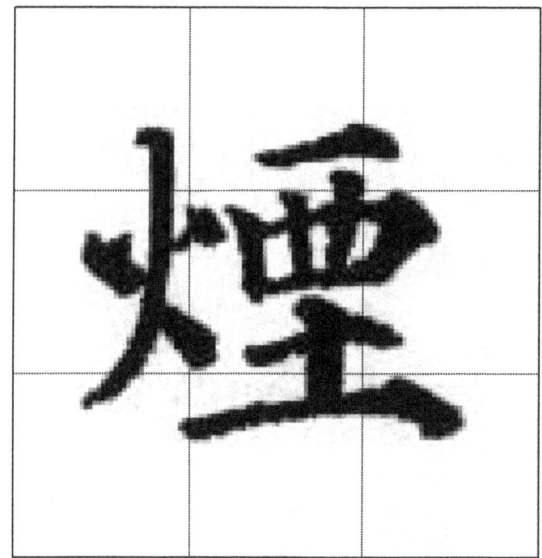

煙=烟/yān/smoke, cigarettes

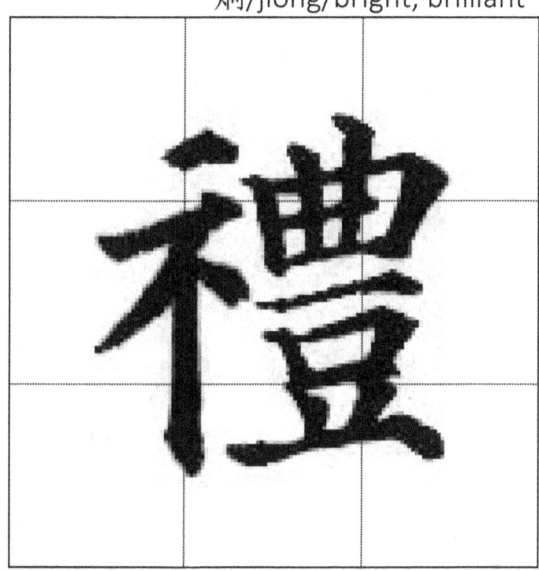

禮=礼/lǐ/gift, ceremony

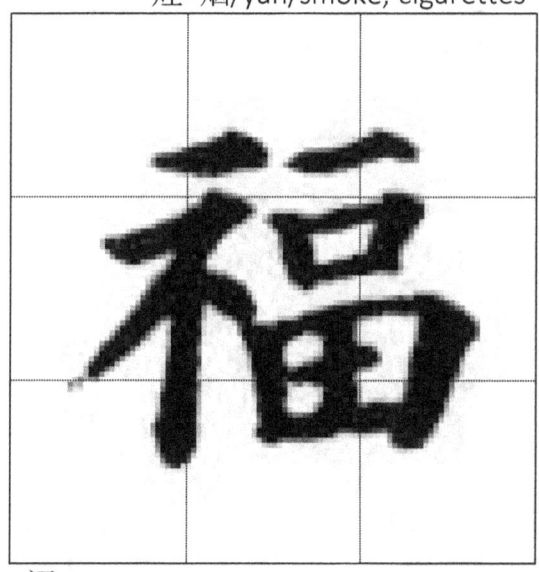

福/fú/happiness, good fortune, blessing

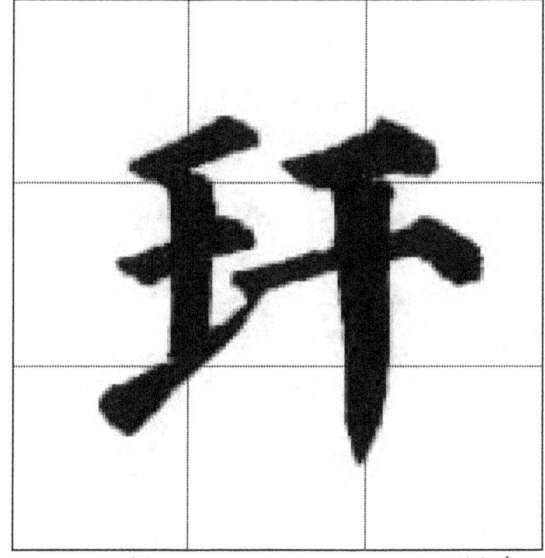

玕/gān/(Part of the word 玕琅)

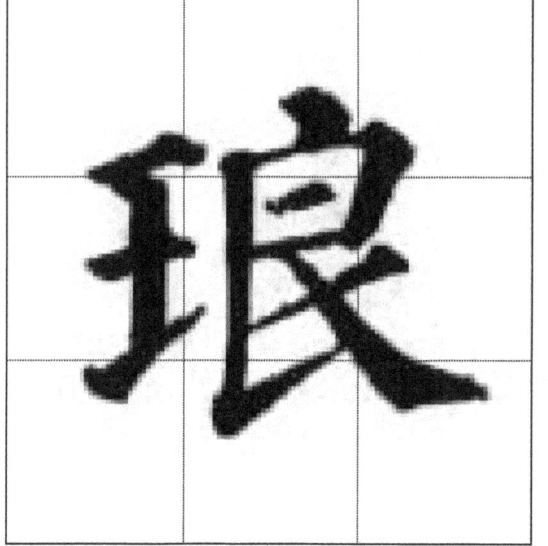

琅/láng/ a variety of white carnelian

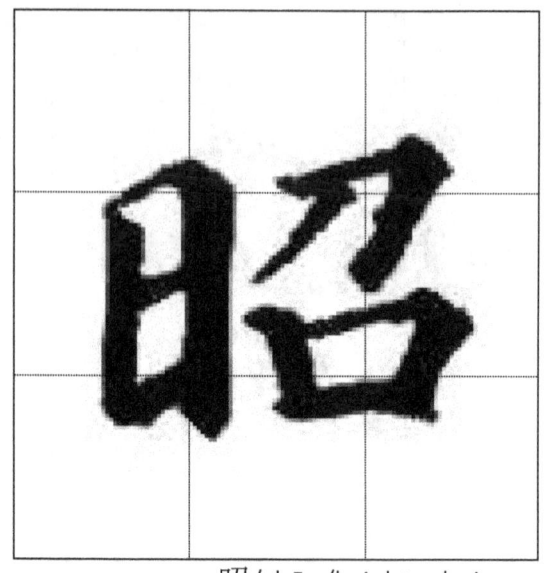

昭/zhāo/bright, obvious

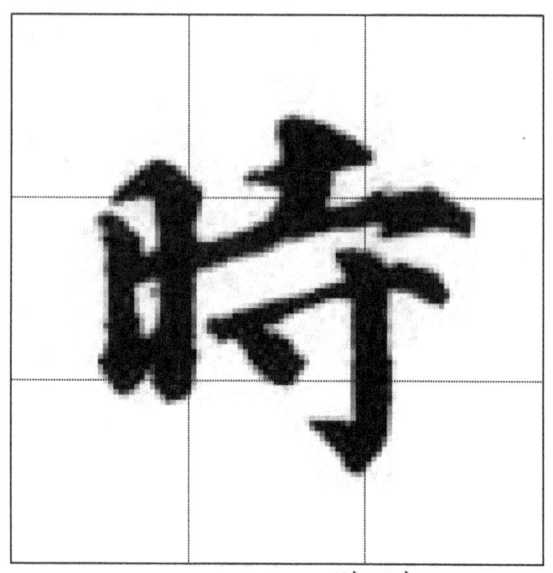

時=时/shí/time

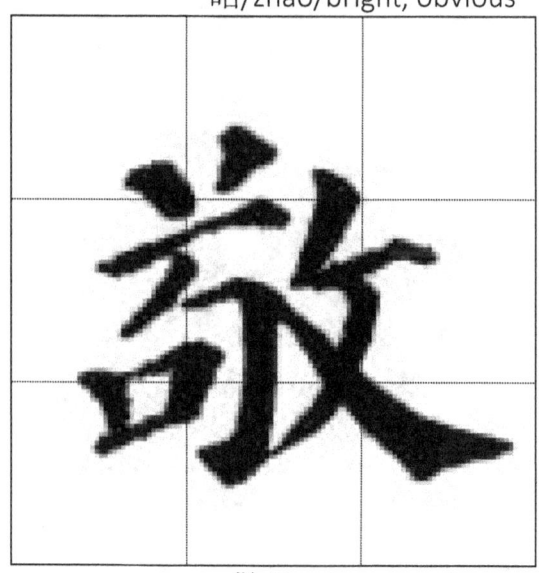

敬/jìng/ respect, honor

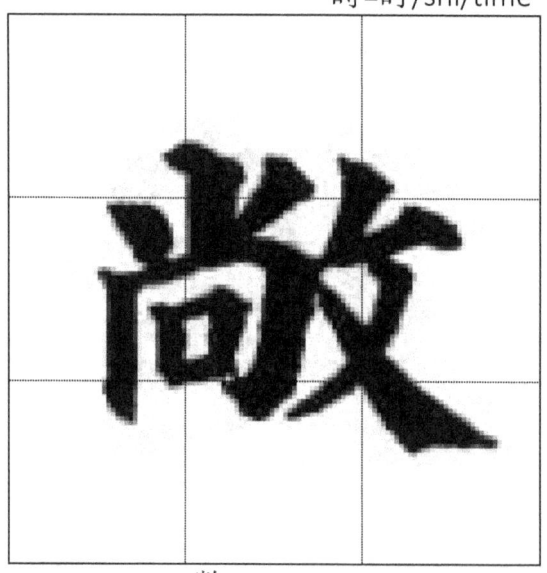

敞/chǎng/ open, spacious

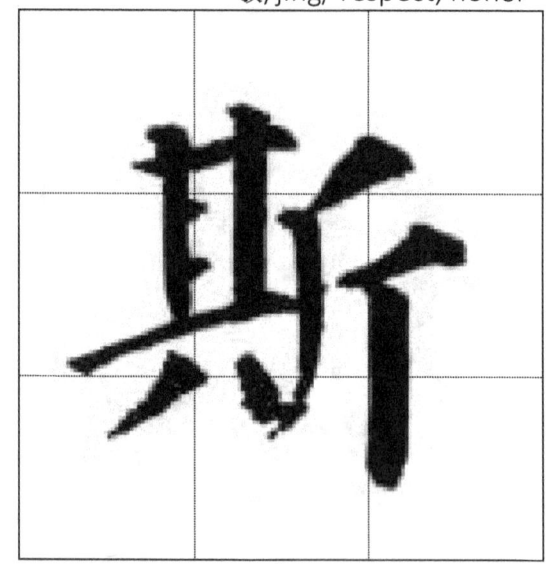

斯/sī/this, thus, such

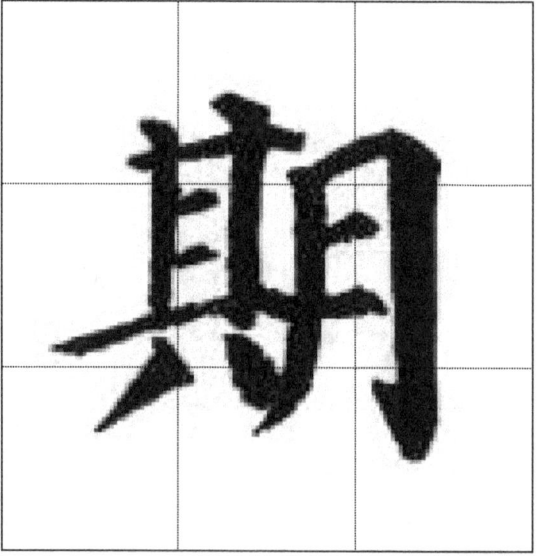

期/qī/a period of time

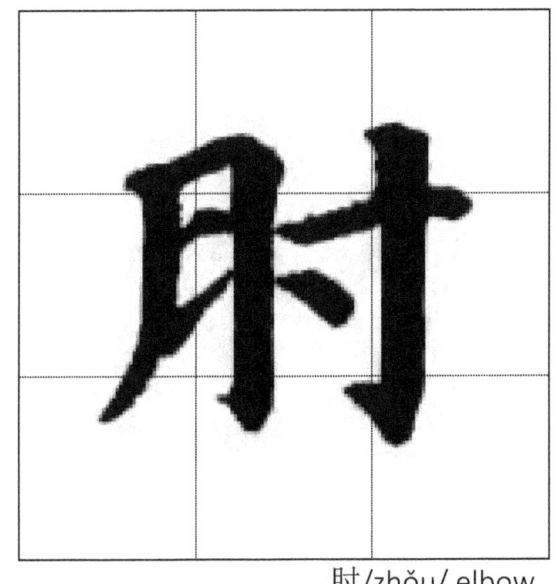

肘/zhǒu/ elbow

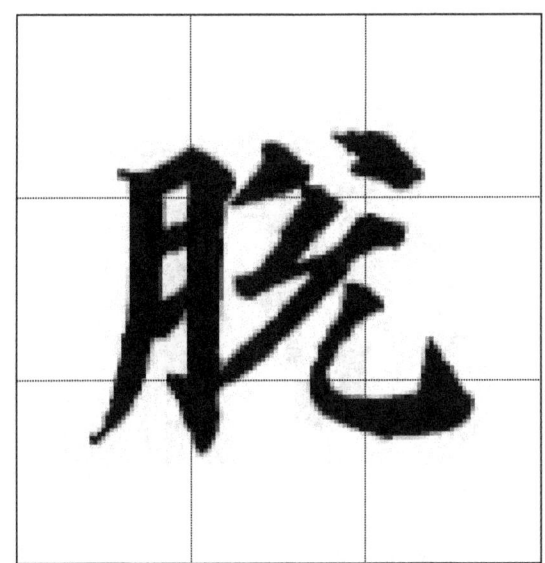

脱/ tuō/take off

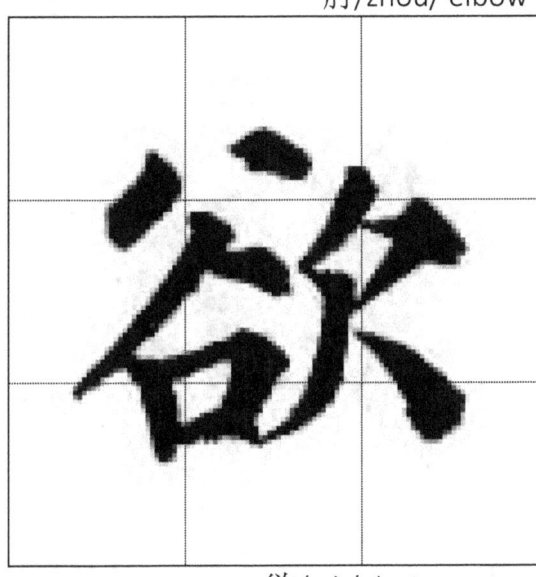

欲/ yù/ desire, want

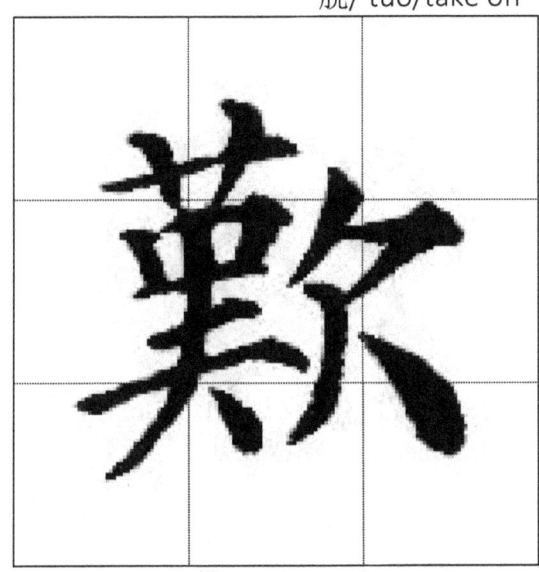

歎＝叹/ tàn/ sigh, admire

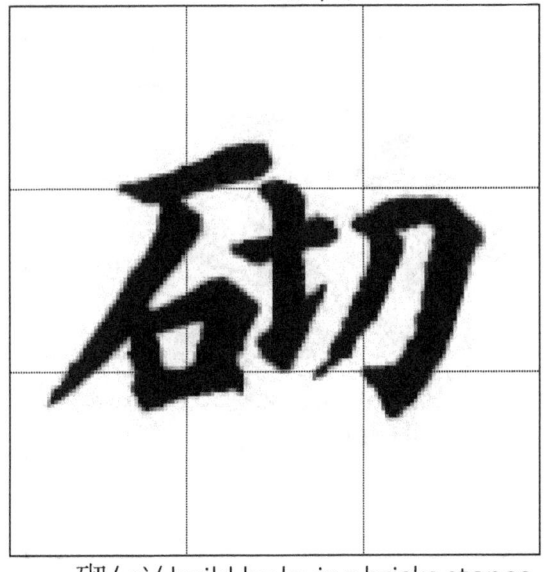

砌/ qì/ build by laying bricks stones

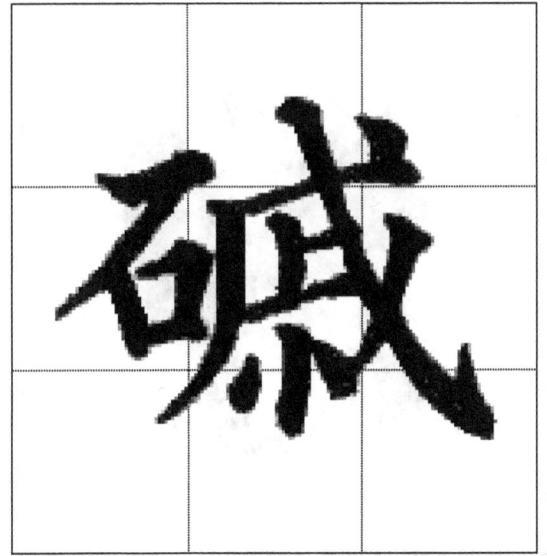

碱/qì/jade-like stone

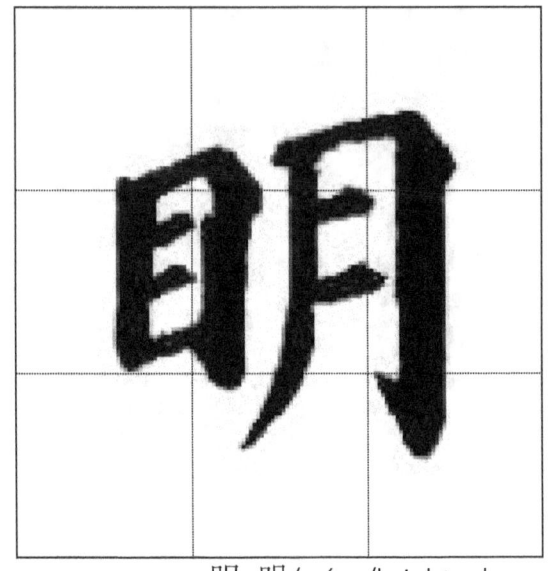

明=明/míng/bright, clear

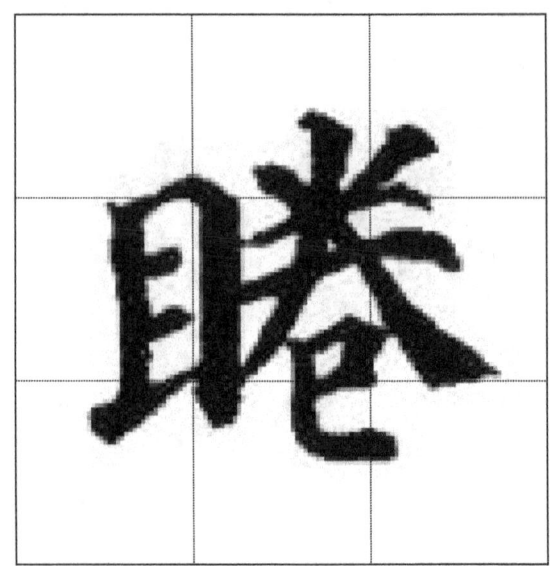

睠=眷/ juàn/ family dependent, care for

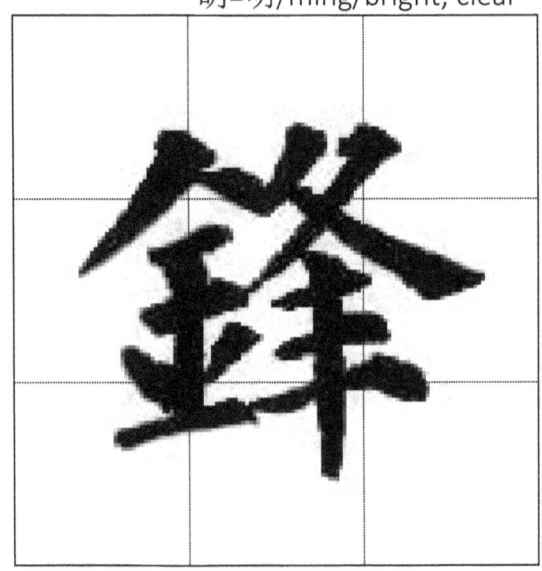

鋒=锋/ fēng/ sharp edge of a sword

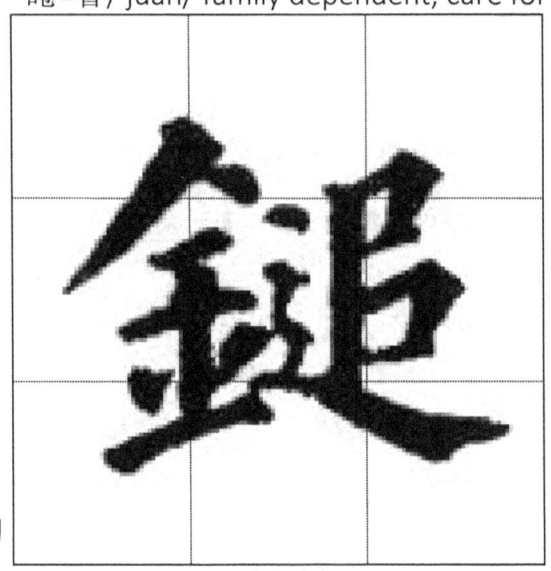

鎚=锤/ chuí/ hammer

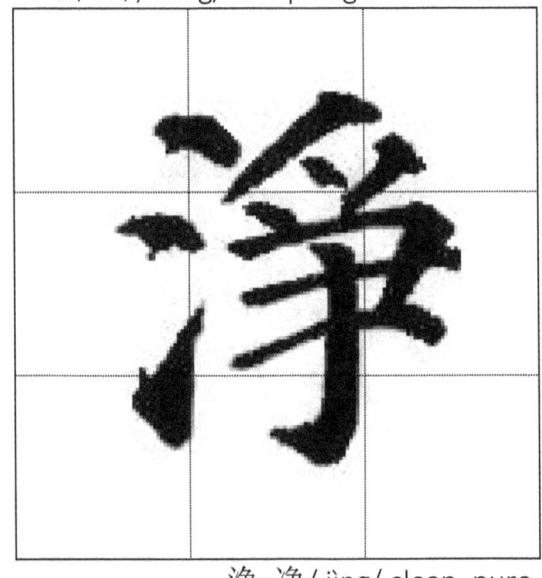

淨=净/ jìng/ clean, pure

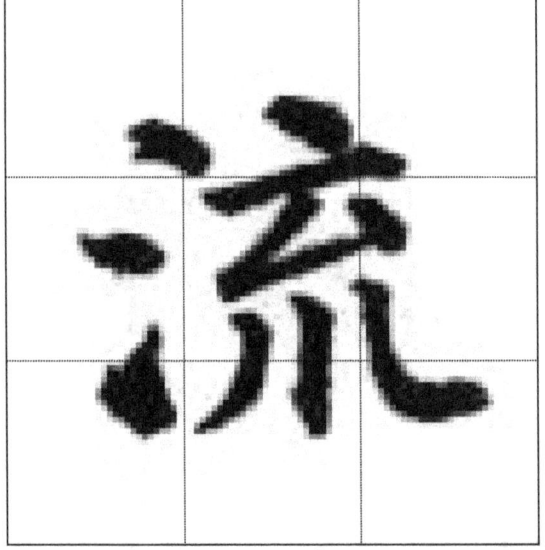

流/ liú/flow, drift

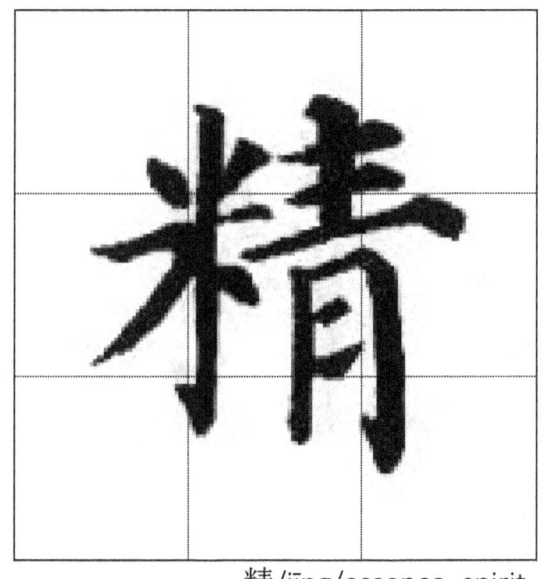

精/jīng/essence, spirit

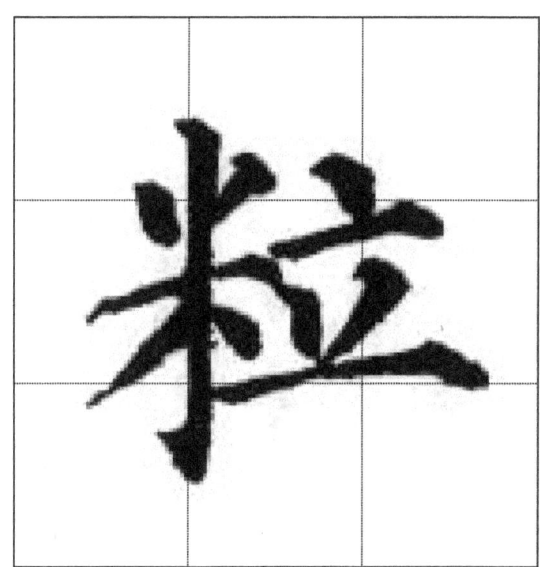

粒/ lì/ grain; small particle

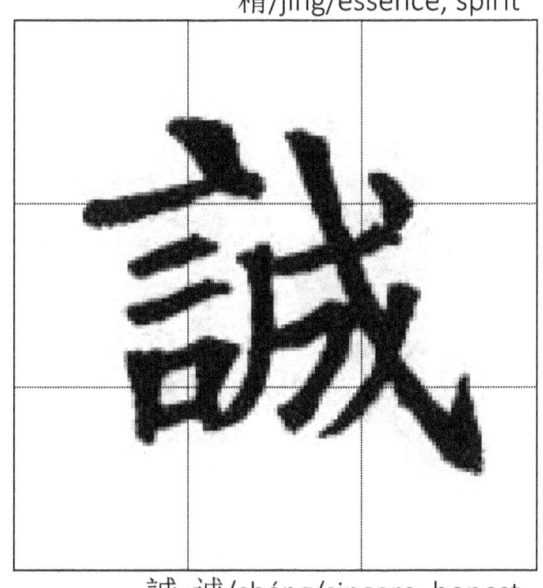

誠=诚/chéng/sincere, honest

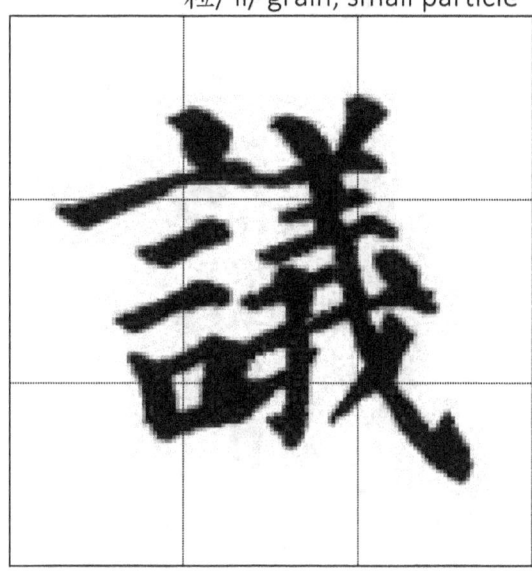

議=议/ yì/ discuss

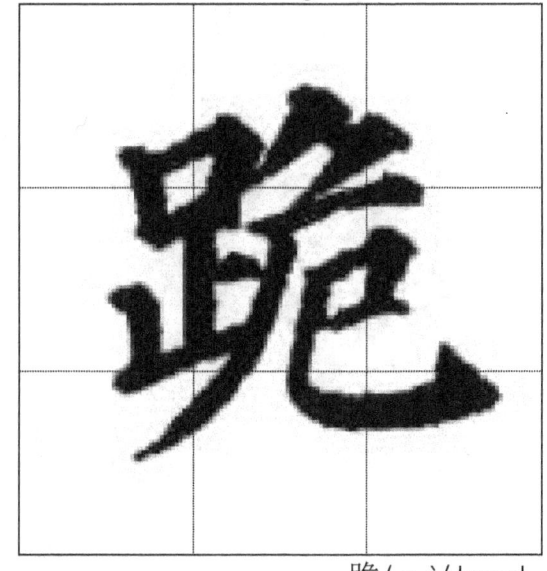

跪/ guì/ kneel

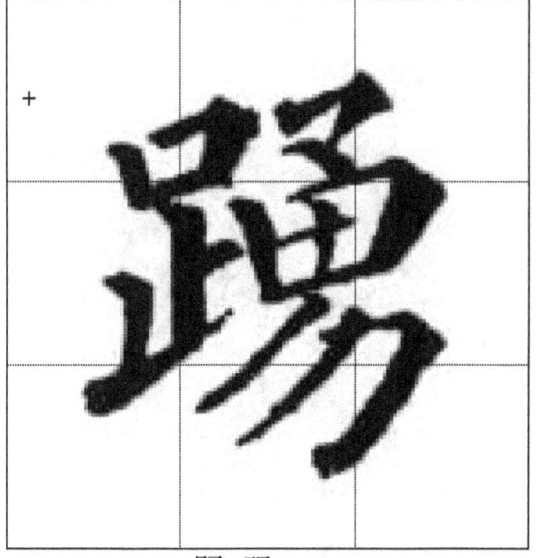

踴=踊/ yǒng/ leap, jump

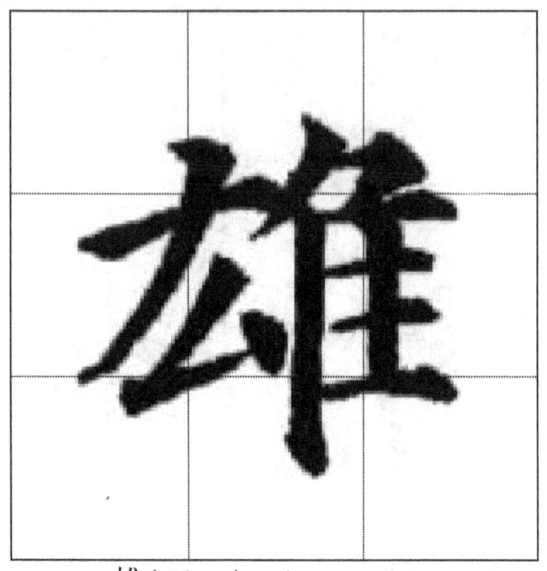

雄/xióng/ male, grand, imposing

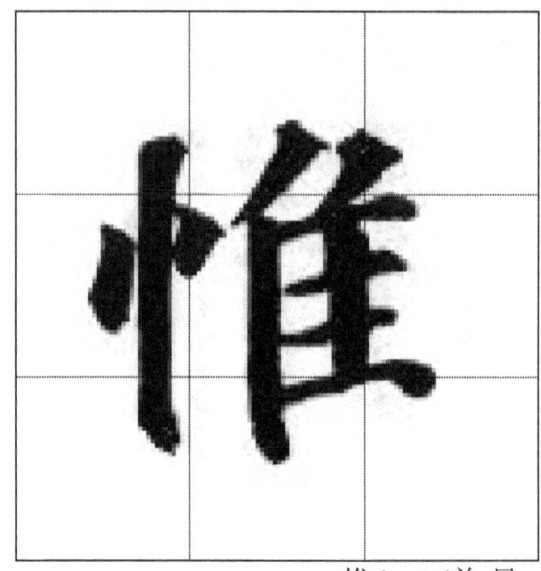

惟/ wéi/单,只

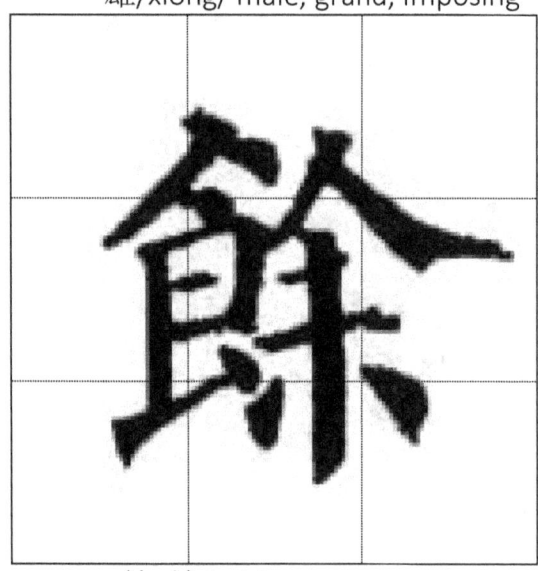

餘=馀/ yú/remaining, I, my, me

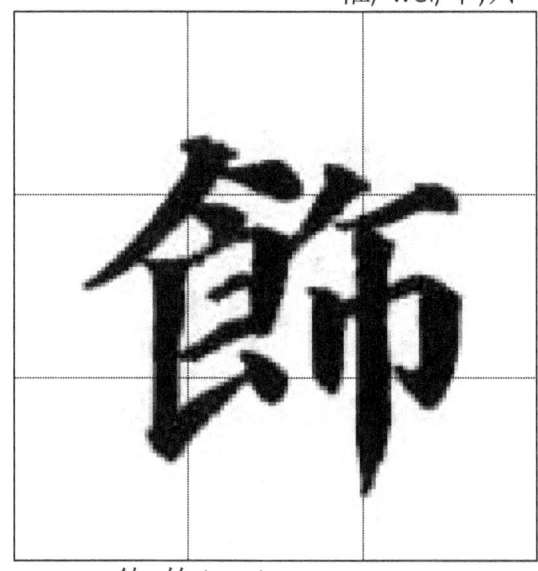

飾=饰/ shì/ decorate, ornament

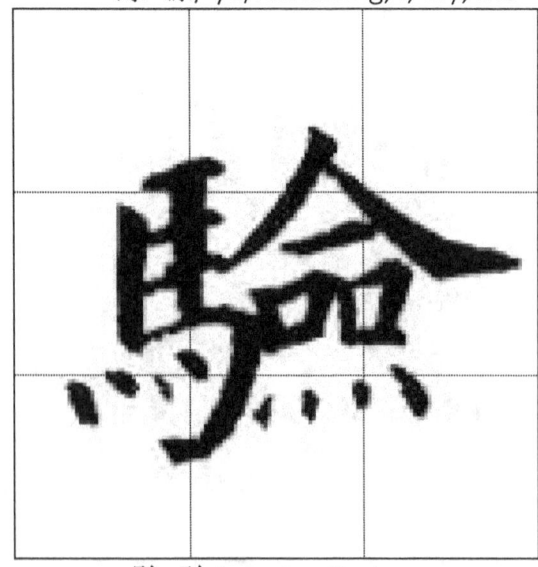

驗=验/ yàn/verify, inspect, test

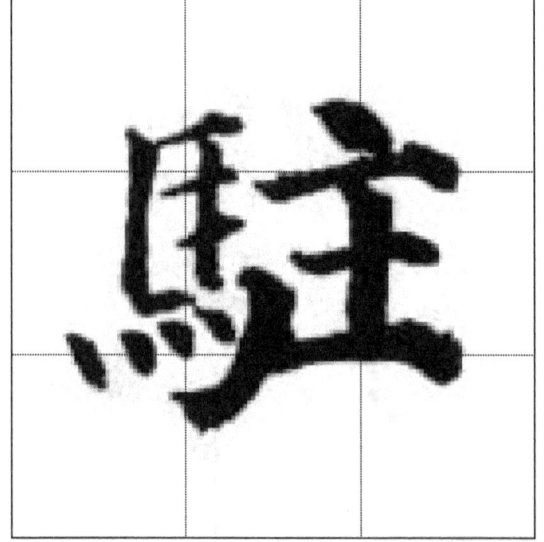

駐=驻/ zhù/ be stationed at, reside at

中国古代名言
Famous Ancient Chinese Sayings

中国古代名言
Famous Ancient Chinese Sayings
1—A

繁体 Traditional Characters	意	在	筆	先
简体 Simplified Characters	意	在	笔	先
拼音 Chinese Phonetics	yì	zài	bǐ	xiān
英语 English Definition	sense	be at	writing brush	before
翻译 English Translation	Conceive before you move your brush;			

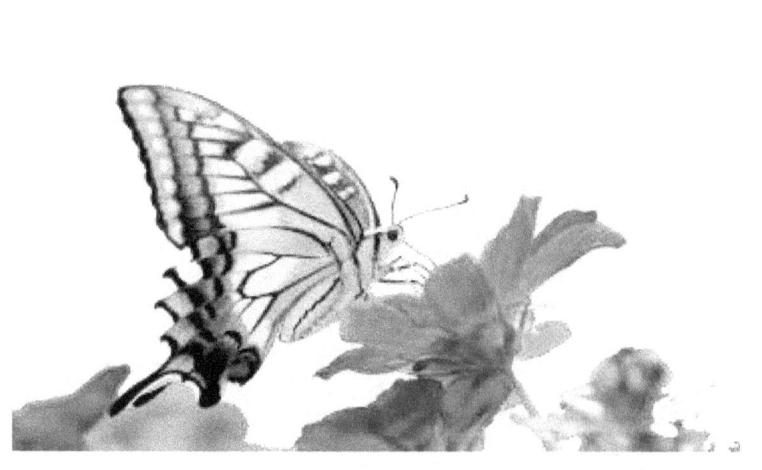

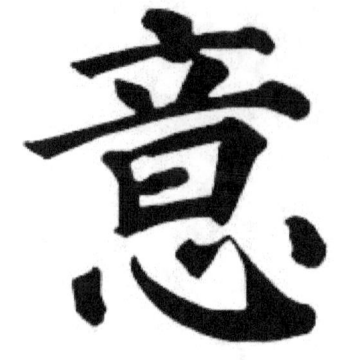

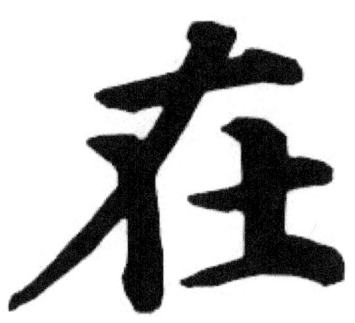

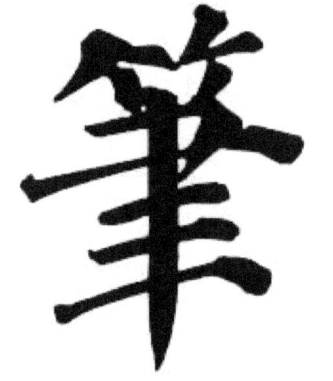

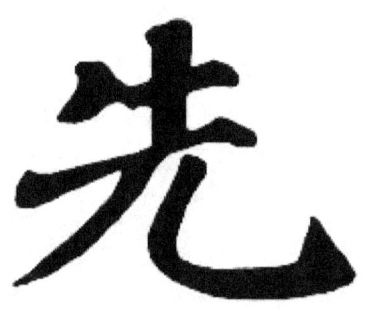

中国古代名言
Famous Ancient Chinese Sayings
1—B

繁体 Traditional Characters	然	後	書	寫
简体 Simplified Characters	然	后	书	写
拼音 Chinese Phonetics	rán	hòu	shū	xiě
英语 English Definition	later		to write	
翻译 English Translation:	Then begin to apply your brush.			
出处 Source:	王羲之《题笔阵图后》/*The Inscription of Bi Zhen Tu* by Wang Xizhi			

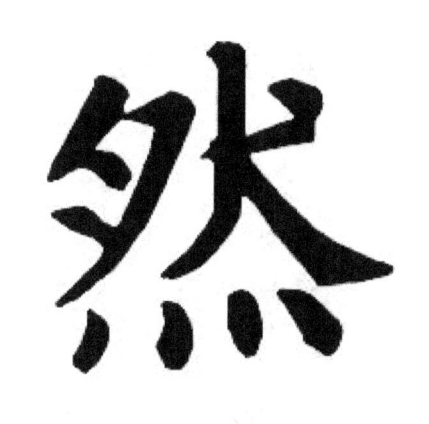

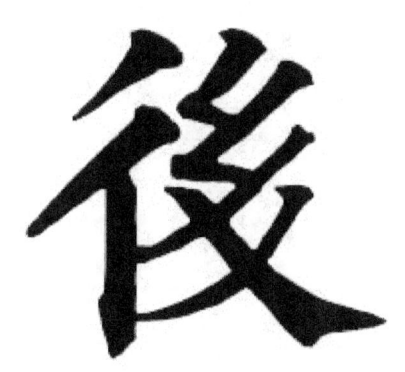

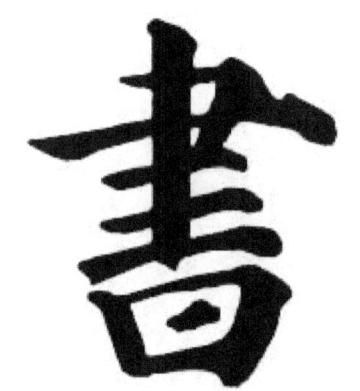

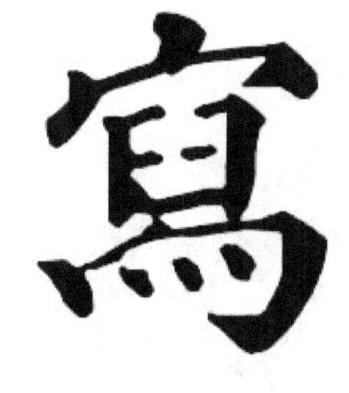

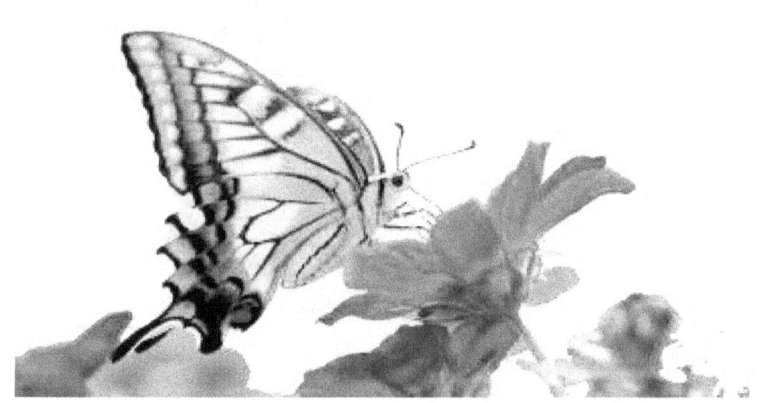

中国古代名言
Famous Ancient Chinese Sayings
2

繁体 Traditional Characters:	初	學	臨	書
简体 Simplified Characters	初	学	临	书
拼音 Chinese Phonetics:	chū	xué	lín	shū
英语 English Definition	first	to study	to imitate	copy book
翻译 English Translation	to imitate first			

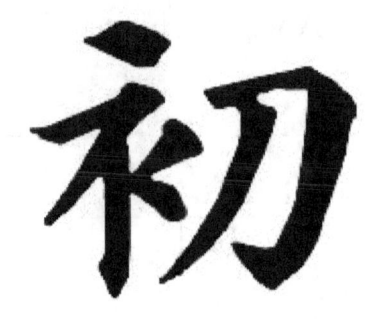
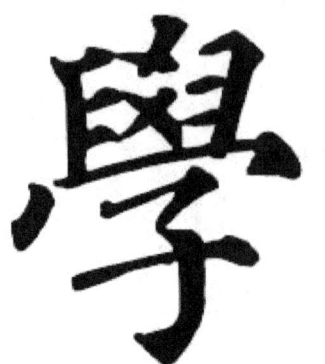
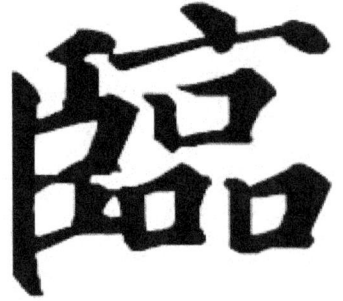
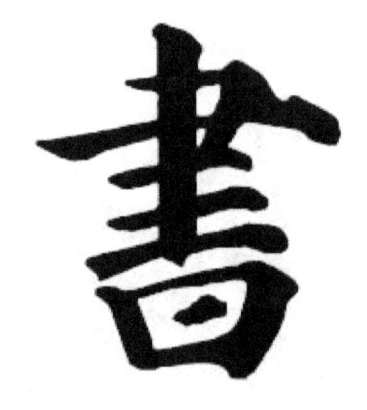

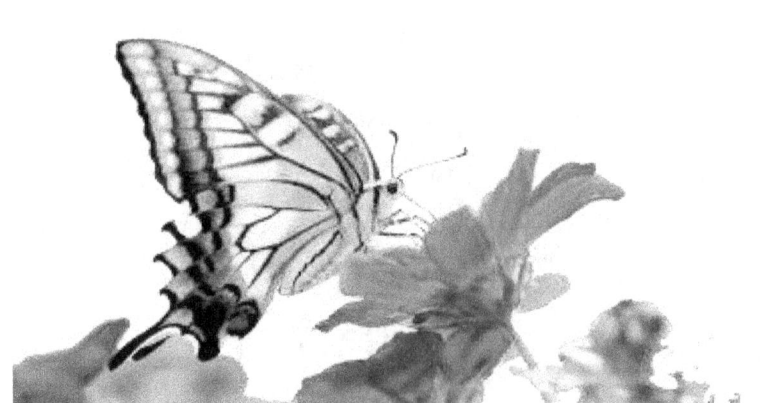

中国古代名言
Famous Ancient Chinese Sayings
3—A

繁体 Traditional Characters	用	筆	在	心
简体 Simplified Characters	用	笔	在	心
拼音 Chinese Phonetics	yòng	bǐ	zài	xīn
英语 English Definition	to use	brush	be at	heart
翻译 English Translation	The brush is governed by your heart;			

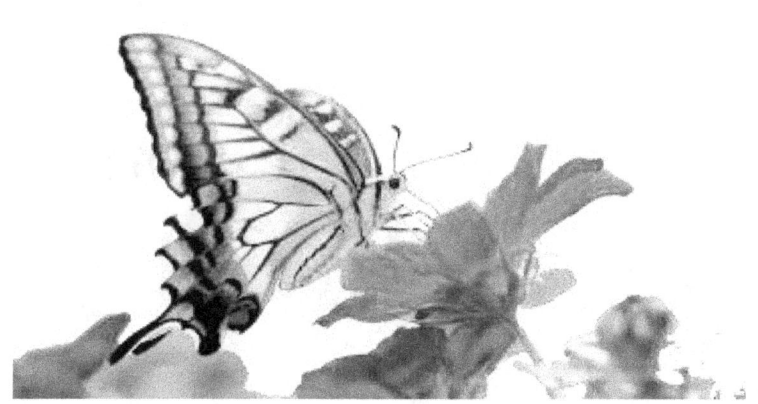

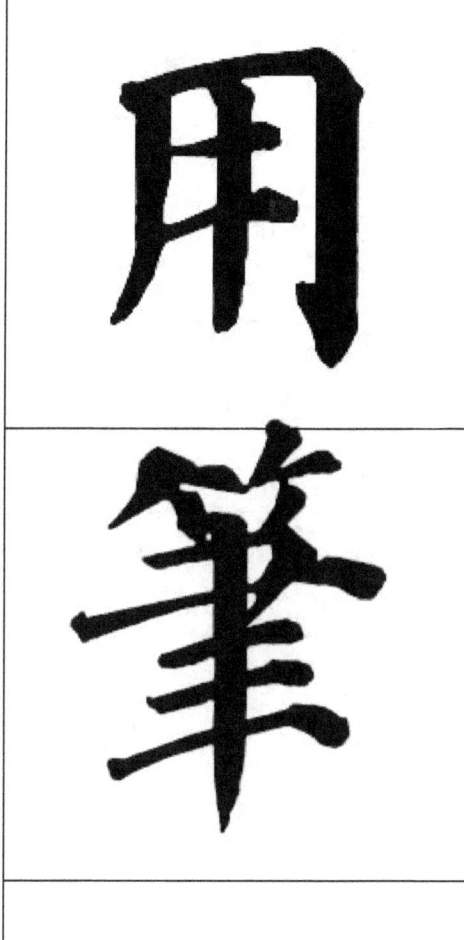

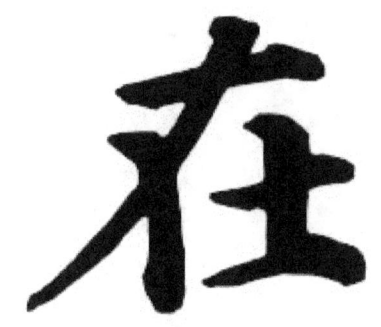

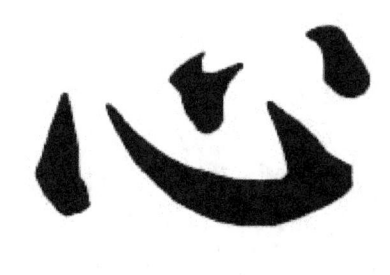

中国古代名言
Famous Ancient Chinese Sayings
3—B

繁体 Traditional Characters	心	正	筆	正
简体 Simplified Characters	心	正	笔	正
拼音 Chinese Phonetics	xīn	zhèng	bǐ	zhèng
英语 English Definition	heart	right	brush	right
翻译 English Translation:	The heart is right, the writing right.			
出处 Source	柳公权/Liu Gongquan			

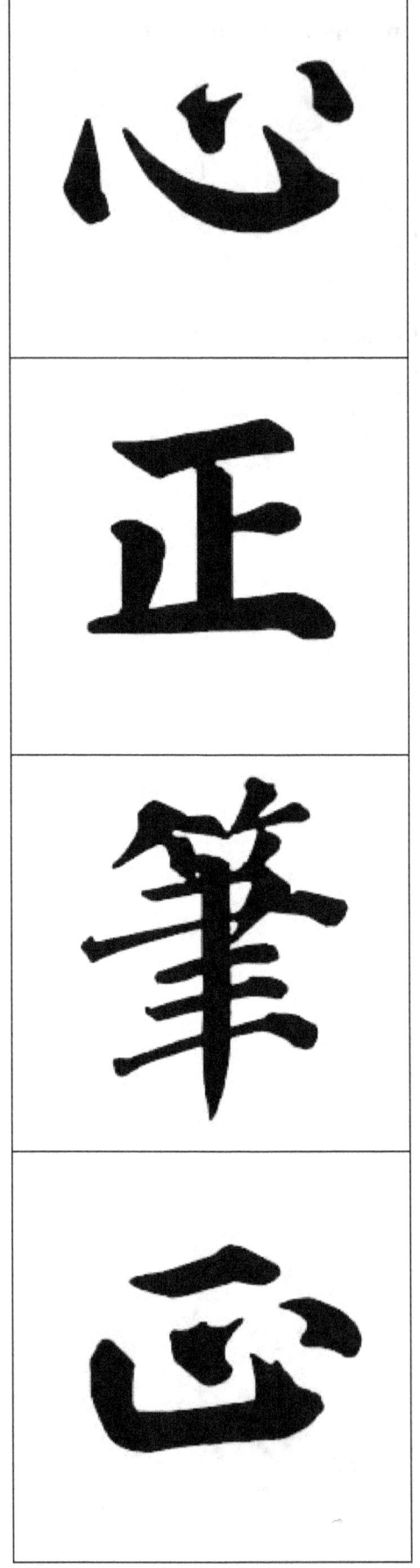

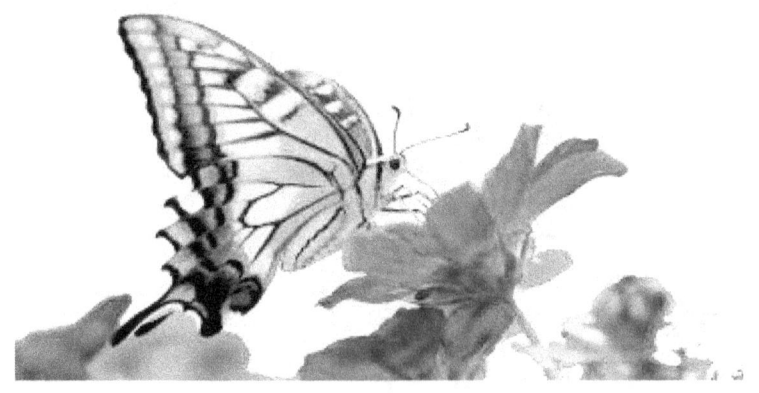

中国古代名言
Famous Ancient Chinese Sayings
4—A

繁体 Traditional Characters	動	雲	龍	之	氣	象
简体 Simplified Characters	动	云	龙	之	气	象
拼音 Chinese Phonetics	dòng	yún	lóng	zhī	qì	xiàng
英语 English Definition	move	clouds	dragon	's	air/atmosphere	
翻译 English Translation:	Possesses the air of a dragon in clouds					

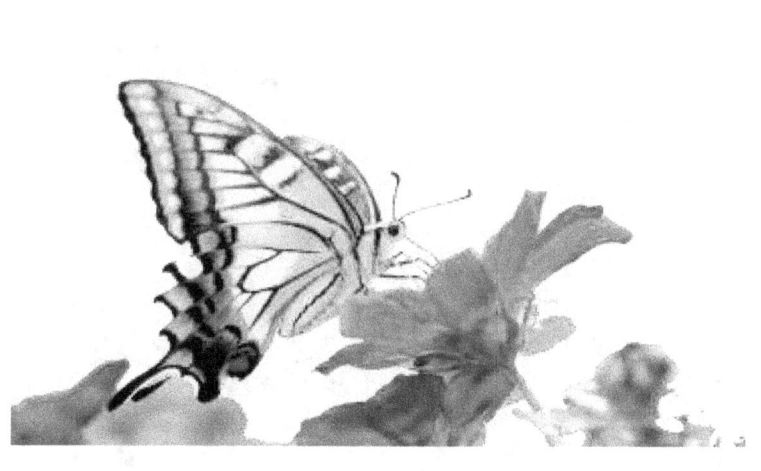

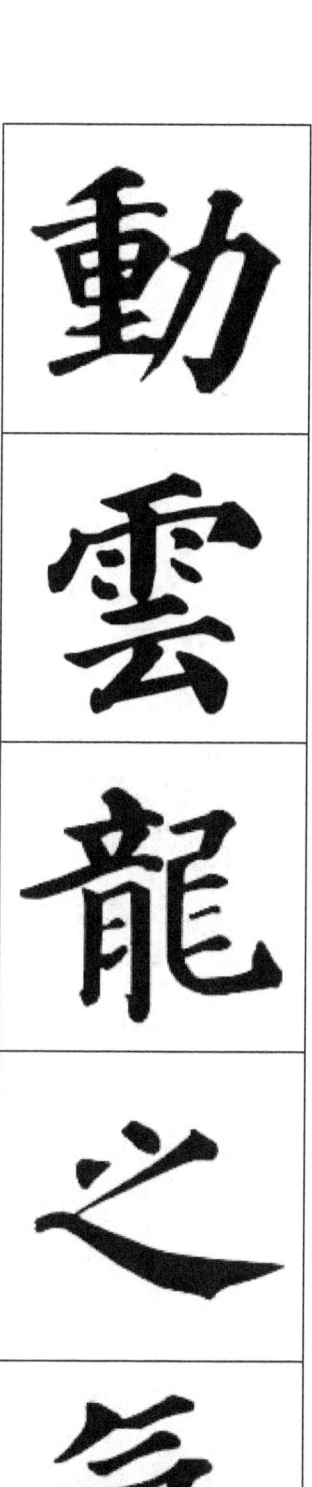

中国古代名言
Famous Ancient Chinese Sayings
4-B

繁体 Traditional Characters	駐	日	月	之	光	輝
简体 Simplified Characters	驻	日	月	之	光	辉
拼音 Chinese Phonetics	zhù	rì	yuè	zhī	guāng	huī
英语 English Definition	to station	sun	moon	's	brilliance	
翻译 English Translation:	retains the brilliance of the sun and the moon					
出处 Source:	颜真卿《多宝塔》/*Duo Bao Ta* by Yan Zhenqing					

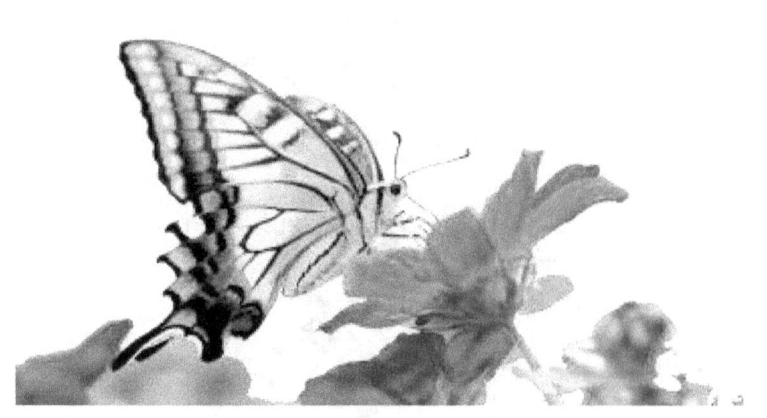

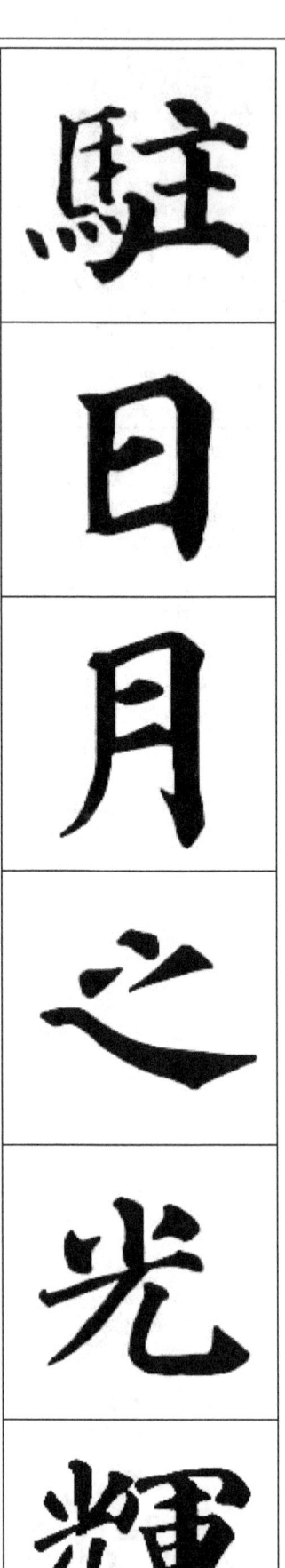

繁体 Traditional Characters	無	聲	之	音
简体 Simplified Characters	无	声	之	音
拼音 Chinese Phonetics	wú	shēng	zhī	yīn
英语 English Definition	no	sound	's	music
翻译 English Translation	Soundless music			

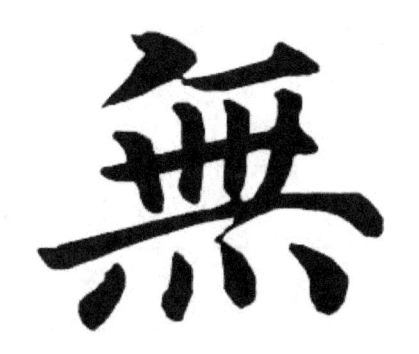
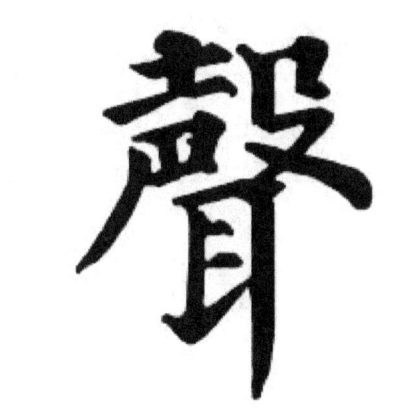
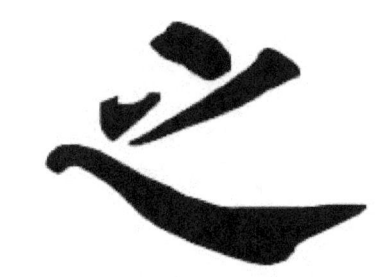
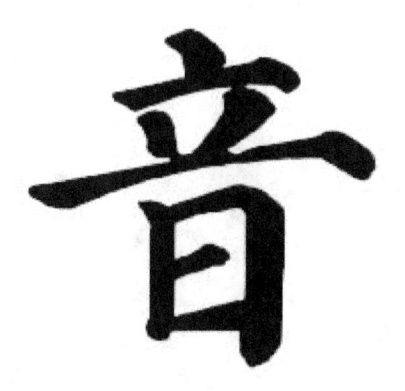

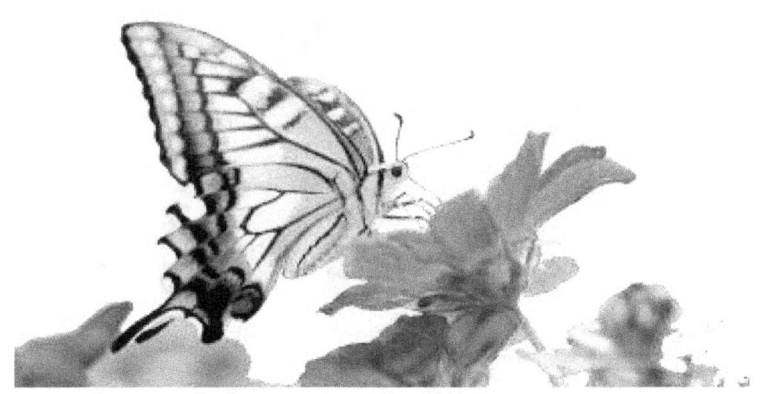

中国古代名言
Famous Ancient Chinese Sayings
6—A

繁体 Traditional Characters	千	里	之	行
简体 Simplified Characters	千	里	之	行
拼音 Chinese Phonetics	qiān	lǐ	zhī	xíng
英语 English Definition	a thousand	miles	's	trip
翻译 English Translation	A trip of a thousand miles			

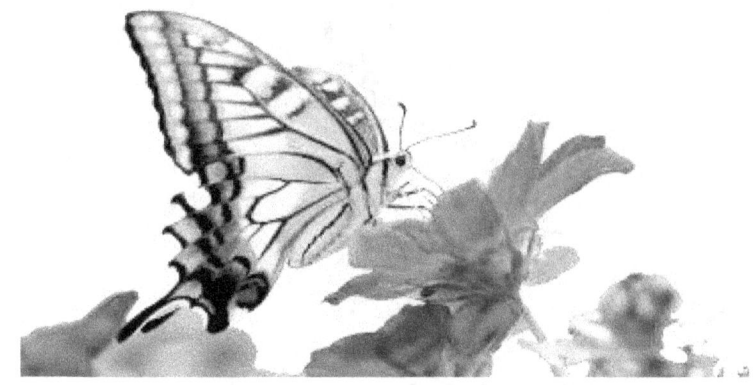

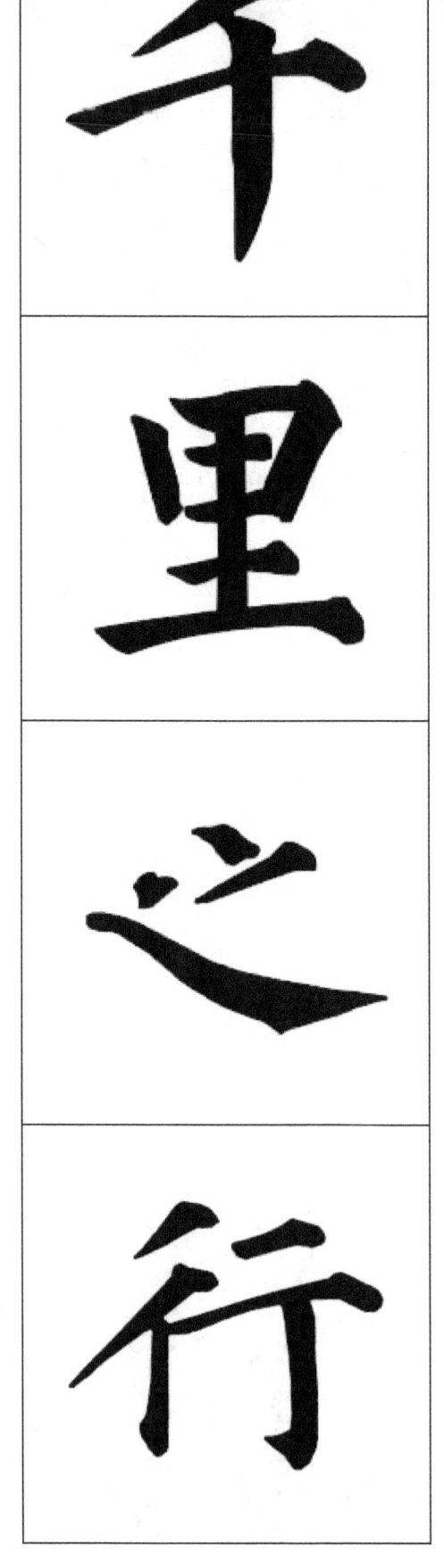

中国古代名言
Famous Ancient Chinese Sayings
6—B

繁体 Traditional Characters	始	于	足	下
简体 Simplified Characters	始	于	足	下
拼音 Chinese Phonetics	shǐ	yú	zú	xià
英语 English Definition	begin	from	under the feet	
翻译 English Translation:	begins with a single step			
出处 Source	老子《道德经》/*Dao De Jing* by Lao Zi			

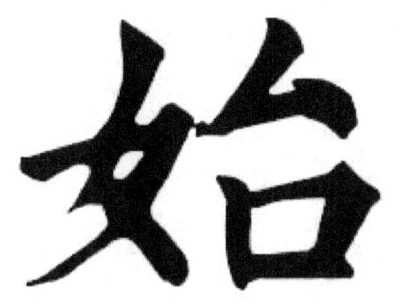

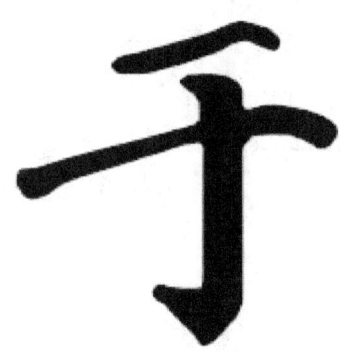

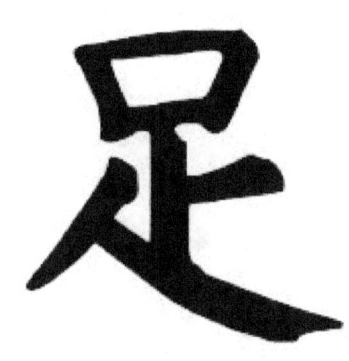

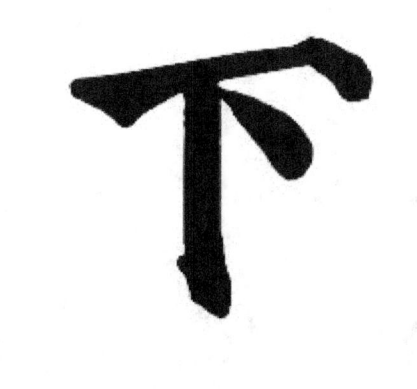

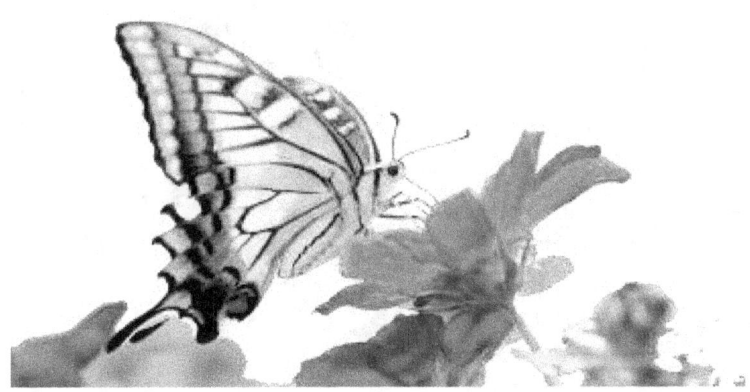

中国古代名言
Famous Ancient Chinese Sayings

7

繁体 Traditional Characters	學	而	不	厭
简体 Simplified Characters	学	而	不	厌
拼音 Chinese Phonetics	xué	ér	bù	yàn
英语 English Definition	to study	but	not	tired
翻译 English Translation :	study tirelessly			
出处 Source	孔子《论语》/ *Lun Yu,* *Analects of Confucius*			

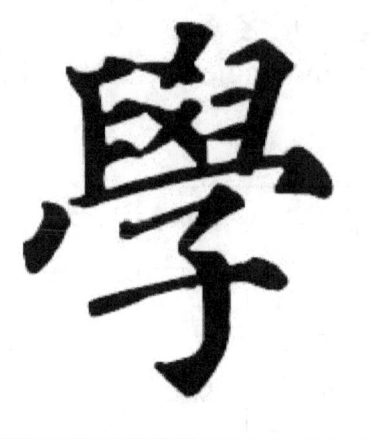

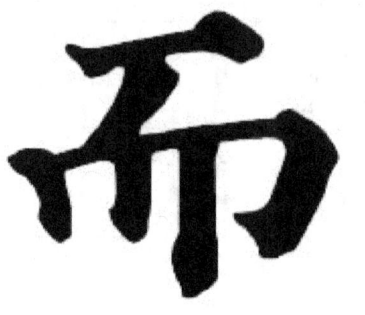

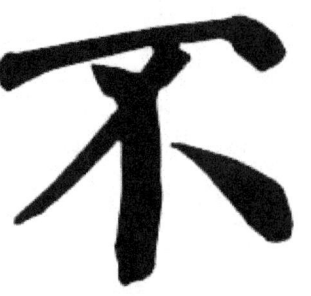

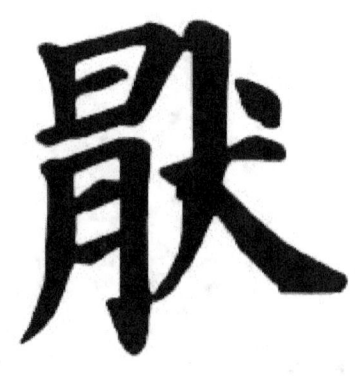

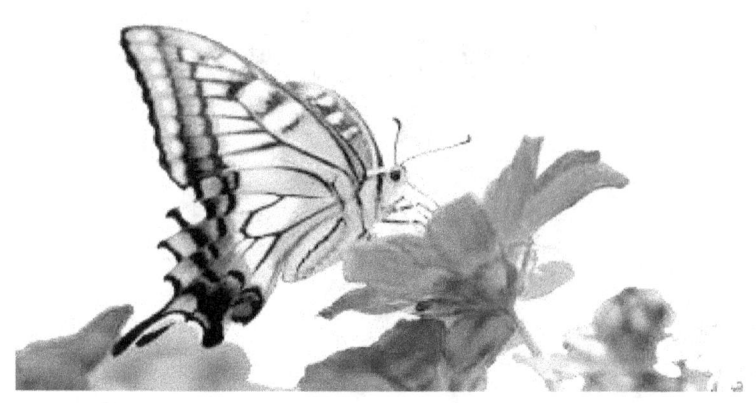

中国古代名言
Famous Ancient Chinese Sayings

8—A

繁体 Traditional Characters	海	納	百	川
简体 Simplified Characters	海	纳	百	川
拼音 Chinese Phonetics	hǎi	nà	bǎi	chuān
英语 English Definition	sea	include	a hundred	river
翻译 English Translation	The sea accepts all rivers;			

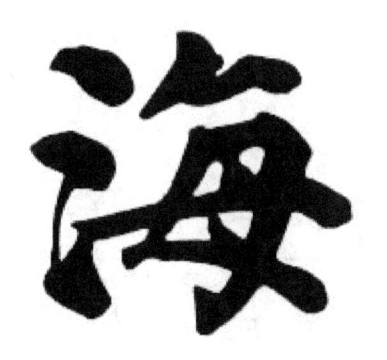
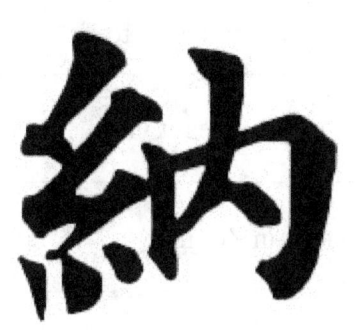
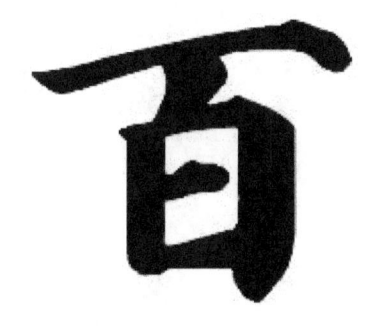
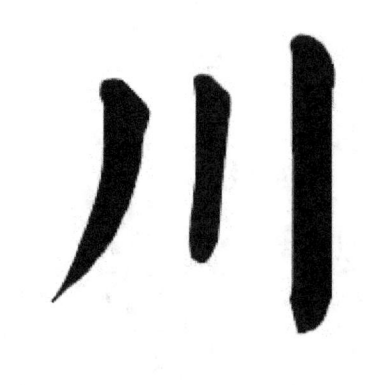
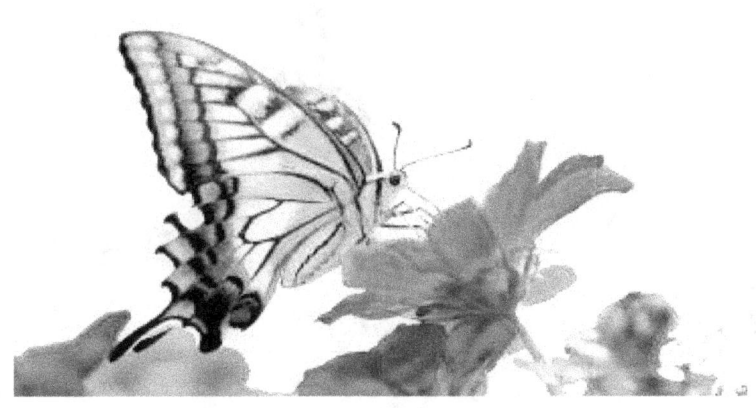

中国古代名言
Famous Ancient Chinese Sayings

8—B

繁体 Traditional Characters	有	容	乃	大
简体 Simplified Characters	有	容	乃	大
拼音 Chinese Phonetics	yǒu	róng	nǎi	dà
英语 English Definition	to have	tolerance	to be	grand
翻译 English Translation:	Tolerance makes it great.			
出处 Source	林则徐/Lin Zexu			

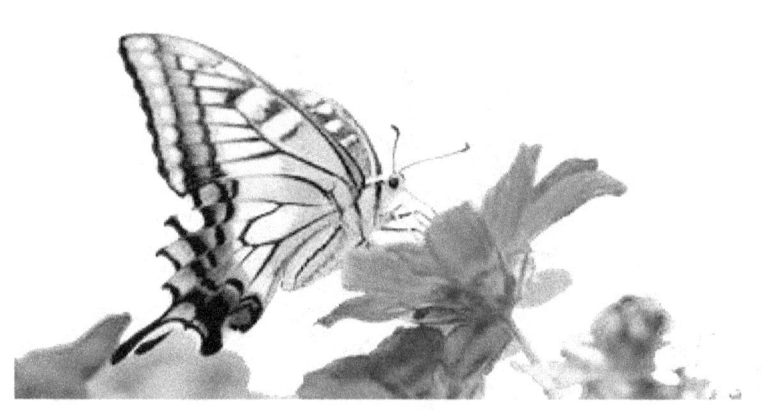

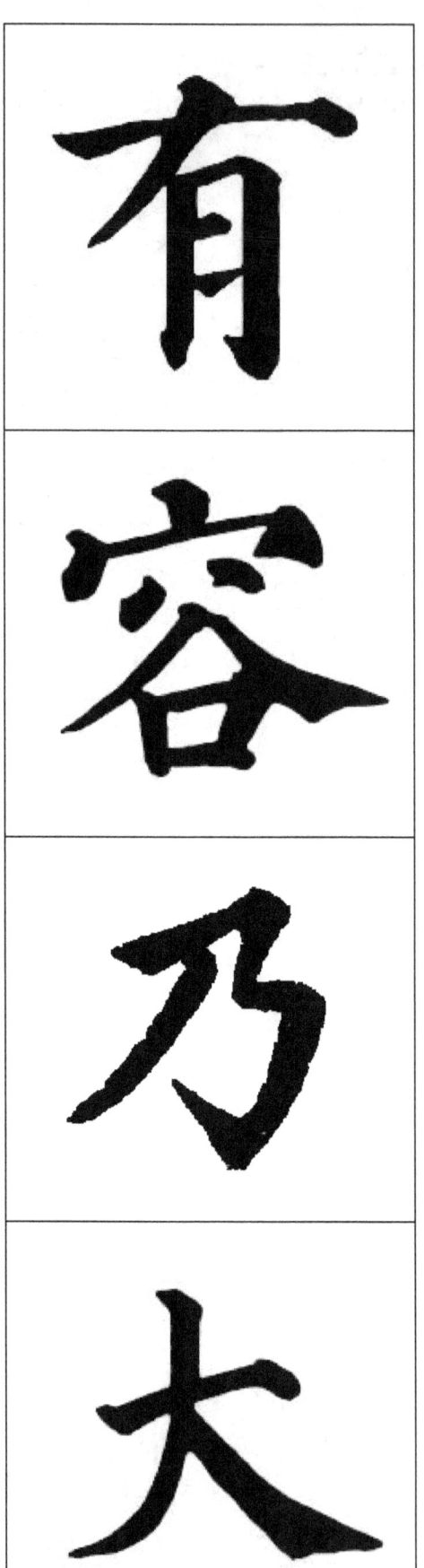

中国古代名言
Famous Ancient Chinese Sayings
9

繁体 Traditional Characters	上	善	若	水
简体 Simplified Characters	上	善	若	水
拼音 Chinese Phonetics	shàng	shàn	ruò	shuǐ
英语 English Definition	best	virtue	be like	water
翻译 English Translation:	The best virtue is like water.			
出处 Source	老子《道德经》/*Dao De Jing* by Lao Zi			

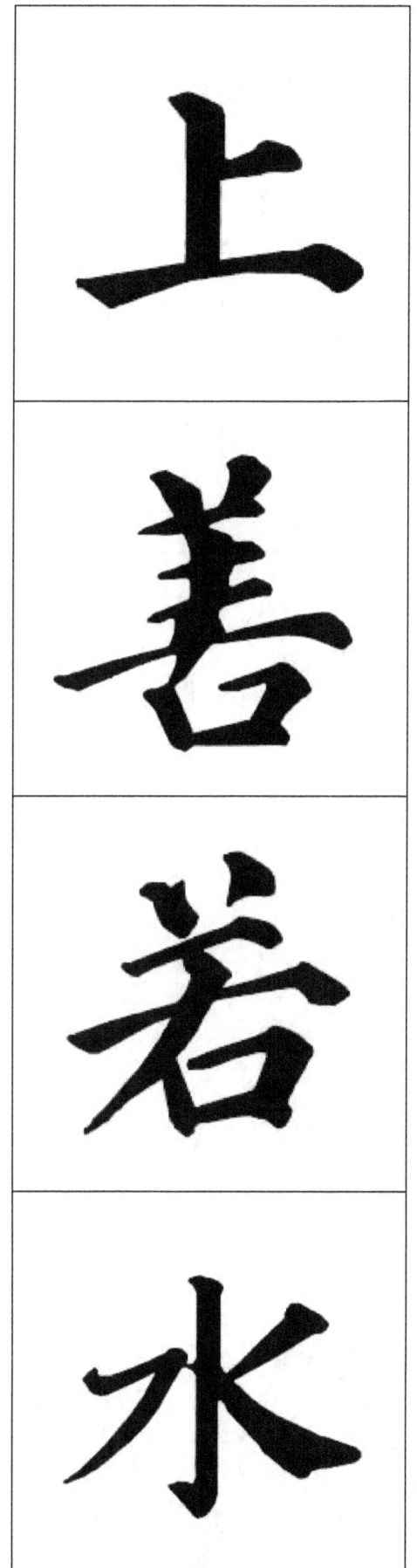

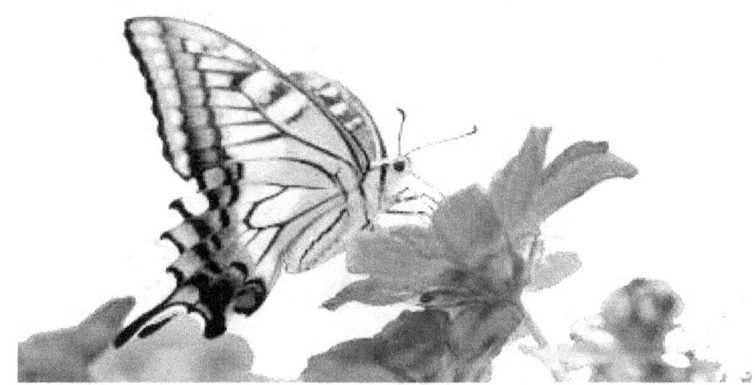

中国古代名言
Famous Ancient Chinese Sayings

10-A

繁体 Traditional Characters	精	誠	所	至
简体 Simplified Characters	精	诚	所	至
拼音 Chinese Phonetics:	jīng	chéng	suǒ	zhì
英语 English Definition	absolute sincerity		where	Reach
翻译 English Translation	Where absolute sincerity reaches,			

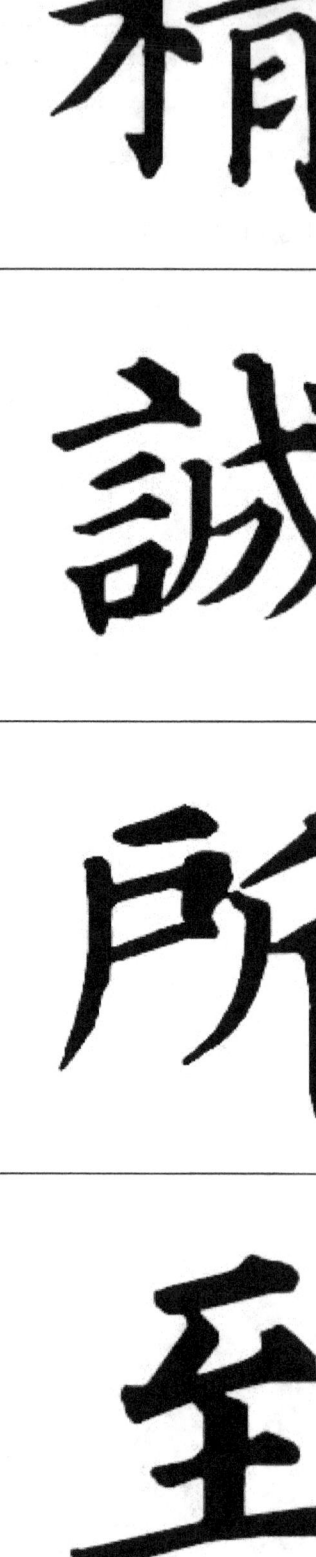

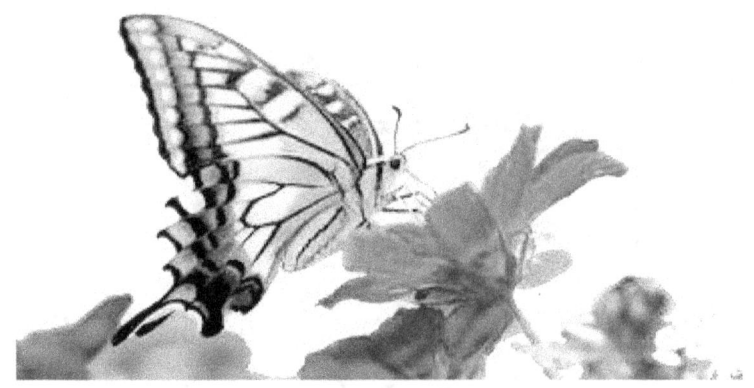

中国古代名言
Famous Ancient Chinese Sayings
10-B

繁体 Traditional Characters	金	石	为	開
简体 Simplified Characters	金	石	为	开
拼音 Chinese Phonetics	jīn	shí	wéi	kāi
英语 English Definition	gold	stone	for sth	open/ bloom
翻译 English Translation:	gold stone will bloom.			
出处 Source	王充《论衡》/*Lunheng* by Wang Chong			

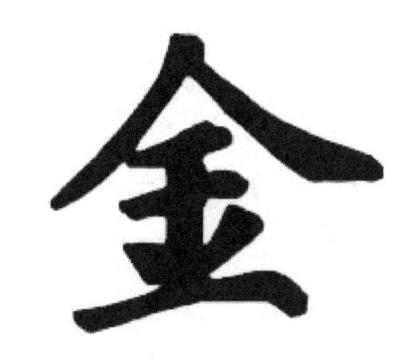

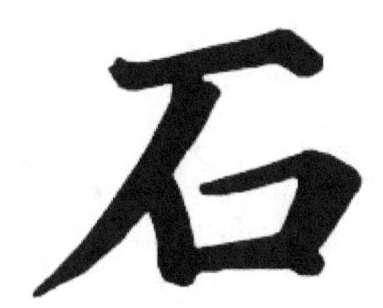

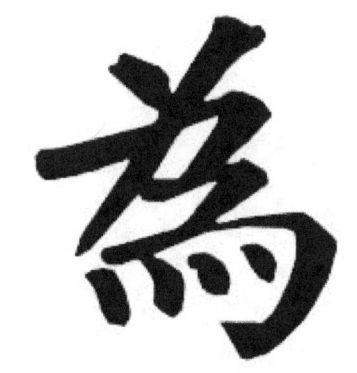

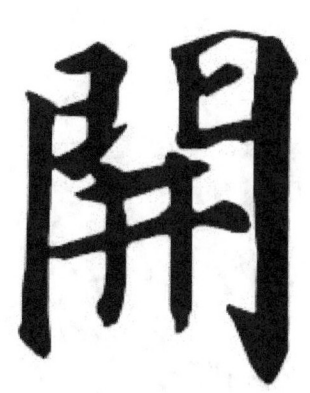

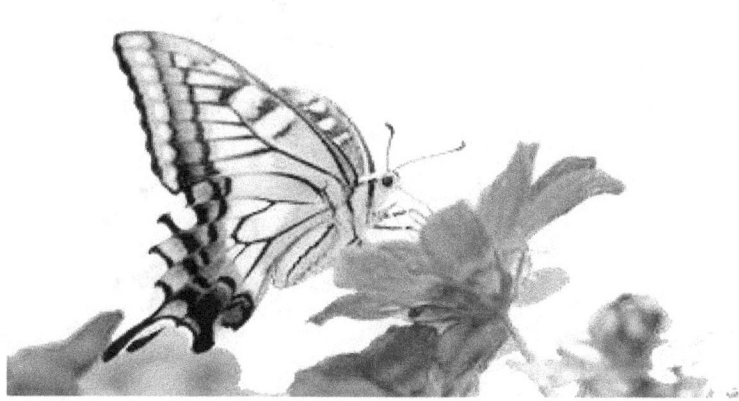

中国古代名言
Famous Ancient Chinese Sayings
11

繁体 Traditional Character	自	强	不	息
简体 Simplified Characters	自	强	不	息
拼音 Chinese Phonetics	zì	qiáng	bù	xī
英语 English Definition	self	strengthen	not	stop
翻译 English Translation	Strengthen yourself without stopping.			
出处 Source	孔子《周易—象传》/ *Book Of Changes* by Confucius			

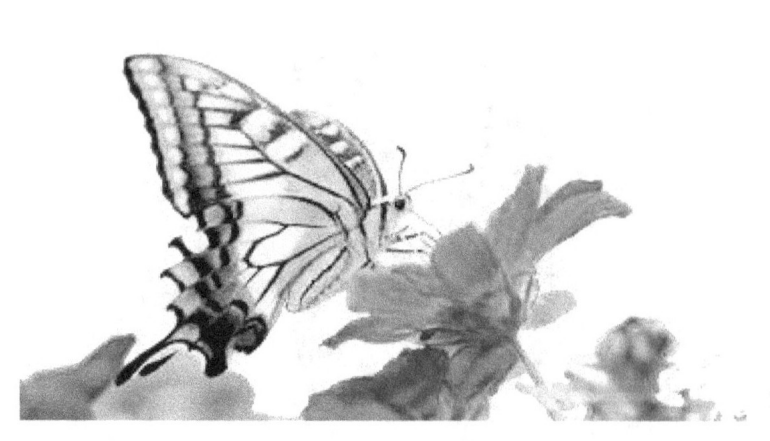

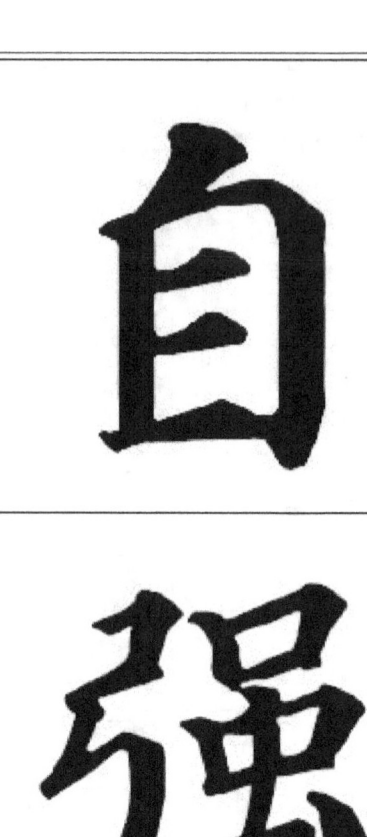

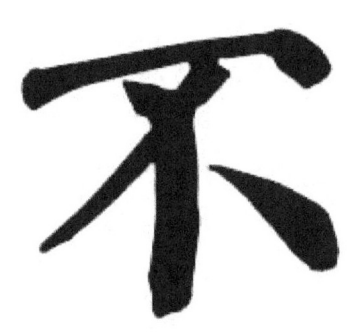

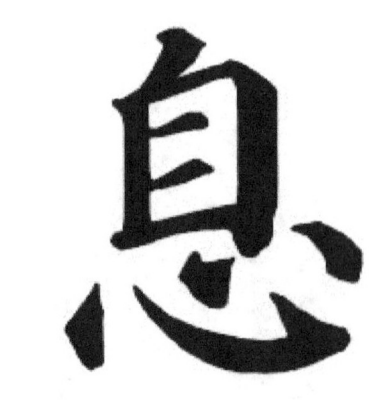